BUILD, SCALE, SELL

HOW YOU CAN BUILD YOUR OWN BUSINESS THAT IS BOTH SCALABLE & SALEABLE

PAUL FLAVIN

Book Design by HMDPUBLISHING

THE FOUR PILLARS TO BUSINESS SUCCESS

Although this book is written through the eyes of Sarah, the owner of a Mortgage Company, the Four Pillars approach isn't just about building a successful business. It's about creating value, fostering growth, and making a positive impact. Whether you're running a company, a tech startup, or a local coffee shop, these principles can transform your business and your life.

"The only limit to our realisation of tomorrow will be our doubts of today"
Franklin D Roosevelt

CONTENTS

CHAPTER 1

THE BUSINESS OWNER'S DILEMMA - SARAH'S JOURNEY

I. The Awakening

Sarah jolted awake, her hand instinctively reaching for her phone before her eyes had fully opened. The pale glow of the screen illuminated her face in the pre-dawn darkness, revealing a flurry of notifications that made her heart sink. Three missed calls from clients, two urgent emails about rate changes, and a reminder about an unpaid invoice. It was 5:30 AM, and Sarah's day as a mortgage broker had already begun.

As she dragged herself out of bed, Sarah caught a glimpse of herself in the mirror. The bags under her eyes told the story of too many late nights and early mornings. At 35, she had achieved her dream of running her own company, but the reality was far from what she had imagined. Instead of the successful, balanced life she had envisioned, she found herself constantly overwhelmed, always racing against the clock, and perpetually worried about the next deal.

Sarah's gaze lingered on a framed photo on her bedside table. It was from her daughter Lily's fifth birthday party, taken just three months ago. Sarah's absence was glaringly obvious in the image - she had been stuck at the office, frantically trying to salvage a deal that was on the brink of falling through. The memory of missing that milestone sent a sharp pang of guilt through her chest. Those missed times with Lily could never be recaptured and she'd sacrificed them for a thing that now seemed irrelevant. What was more important, her daughter or a mortgage application?

As she shuffled towards the bathroom, Sarah's mind drifted back to the path that had led her to this point. The journey from ambitious bank employee to independent mortgage broker had been filled with hope, determination, and unforeseen challenges.

II. The Corporate Ladder: Sarah's Early Career

Sarah's career in the mortgage industry had begun eight years ago when she joined Oakwood Bank as a junior mortgage adviser. Having gained a degree in Finance, she had been drawn to the role by the promise of helping people achieve their dreams of homeownership.

From the very beginning, Sarah had shown a natural aptitude for the work. Her meticulous attention to detail, coupled with a genuine empathy for her clients, quickly set her apart from her peers. She had a knack for explaining complex financial concepts in simple terms, making her popular with first-time buyers who often felt overwhelmed by the mortgage process.

Sarah's superiors took notice of her talents, and her rise through the ranks was swift. Within three years, she had been promoted to Senior Mortgage Adviser, managing a team of junior advisors and handling the bank's most complex cases.

On the surface, Sarah's career at Oakwood Bank was a resounding success. Her salary had nearly doubled since she started, she had a corner office with a view of the city, and she was consistently recognised as one of the top performers in the mortgage division.

Yet, as Sarah stared at her reflection in the bathroom mirror, she remembered the growing sense of dissatisfaction that had begun to gnaw at her during those later years at the bank.

III. The Seeds of Discontent

The first cracks in Sarah's corporate facade had appeared during a routine performance review with her manager, David, five years into her tenure at Oakwood Bank.

"Sarah, your numbers are fantastic as always," David had said, his eyes scanning the report in front of him. "You're one of our top producers, and the customer feedback is consistently excellent."

Sarah had smiled, waiting for the 'but' that she sensed was coming.

"However," David continued, confirming her suspicion, "I'm a bit concerned about your adherence to our new sales scripts. Those higher-up are really pushing for standardisation across all customer interactions."

Sarah felt a familiar frustration bubbling up inside her. "David, those scripts don't work for every client. Each case is unique, and I find I get better results when I can tailor my approach."

David had sighed, leaning back in his chair. "I understand, Sarah. But you must see the bigger picture. We're a large institution, and consistency is key. We need to be able to measure and replicate success across the board."

As Sarah had left David's office that day, she felt a weight settling on her shoulders. The conversation had crystallised a feeling she'd been grappling with for months - a sense that the corporate machine was slowly squeezing the humanity out of her work.

Over the next few weeks, Sarah found herself increasingly frustrated by the constraints of her role. The scripted interactions felt robotic and impersonal. The pressure to push certain products, regardless of whether they were the best fit for the client, grated against her personal ethics.

One particularly difficult day stood out in Sarah's memory. A young couple, first-time buyers with a complex income situation, had come to her for help. Sarah knew she could find a solution for them, but it would require thinking outside the box and potentially looking beyond Oakwood Bank's product range.

As she had begun to explore options with the couple, her manager had interrupted the meeting.

"Sarah, can I have a quick word?" David had asked, gesturing for her to step outside.

In the hallway, David's expression was stern. "I overheard you discussing other lenders with that couple. You know our policy - we only recommend Oakwood products unless there's absolutely no other option."

Sarah had felt her face flush with a mix of embarrassment and anger. "But David, our products aren't the best fit for their situation. If we force them into something that doesn't work, they could end up in financial difficulty down the line."

David's response had been curt. "That's not our concern, Sarah. Our job is to sell Oakwood products. If they don't fit, then maybe they're not the right clients for us."

As Sarah had watched the disappointed couple leave the bank empty-handed later that day, she felt a deep sense of disillusionment. This wasn't why she had gotten into the mortgage industry. She wanted to help people, not push products that weren't right for them.

That night, as Sarah lay in bed, unable to sleep, the idea of going independent first crossed her mind. It was a fleeting thought at first, quickly dismissed as too risky. But over the coming months, as similar scenarios played out again and again, the idea began to take root.

IV. The Decision to Leave

The final straw came on a sunny Tuesday afternoon, almost exactly six years into Sarah's career at Oakwood Bank. She had been called into an emergency meeting with the entire mortgage team.

The bank's CEO, a stern-faced man Sarah had only seen from afar at company events, stood at the front of the conference room.

"Ladies and gentlemen," he began, his voice carrying an undercurrent of barely contained excitement, "I have some incredible news. Oakwood Bank has just finalised a merger with Hampshire Group. This positions us to become the largest mortgage lender in the country!"

A murmur of surprise rippled through the room. Sarah felt a knot forming in her stomach.

The CEO continued, outlining the changes that would come with the merger. Expanded product lines, aggressive growth targets, and a new, even more rigid sales structure were all part of the plan.

As the meeting progressed, Sarah found it increasingly difficult to breathe. The vision being laid out before her was a far cry from the reason she had joined the industry. The focus was entirely on numbers, market share, and profit margins. There was not a single mention of customer wellbeing or ethical lending practices.

When the meeting finally ended, Sarah stumbled out of the conference room in a daze. She made her way to the ladies' room, locked herself in a cubicle, and let out a quiet sob. This wasn't just a job for her - it was a vocation. She genuinely cared about her clients and wanted to help them make one of the most significant financial decisions of their lives. But in the face of this corporate behemoth, her values seemed hopelessly naive.

That evening, as Sarah sat at her kitchen table long after her husband James and daughter Lily had gone to bed, she made the decision that would change the course of her life. She was going to leave Oakwood Bank and start her own company.

The decision didn't come easily. Sarah spent hours poring over her finances, researching the requirements for independent brokers, and trying to envision what her life might look like if she took this leap. The risks were significant - she would be giving up a stable salary, excellent benefits, and a clear career trajectory. But the potential rewards - the freedom to truly help her clients, to build something of her own - seemed worth the risk.

As the first light of dawn began to creep through the kitchen window, Sarah finally went to bed. For the first time in months, she fell asleep with a sense of purpose and excitement for the future.

V. The Leap into Self-Employment

The next few months were a whirlwind of activity for Sarah. She threw herself into preparations for her new venture with the same determination and attention to detail that had made her successful at Oakwood Bank.

Evenings and weekends were spent studying for the additional qualifications she would need as an independent broker. She pored over business books, learning about everything from marketing to accounting. Her dining room table disappeared under a sea of papers, folders, and post-it notes.

James, her husband, was supportive but concerned. "Are you sure about this, love?" he asked one night as Sarah worked late into the evening on her business plan. "It's a big risk."

Sarah had looked up from her laptop, her eyes bright with a passion James hadn't seen in years. "I know it's a risk, James. But I have to try. I can't keep working in a system that doesn't align with my values. This is my chance to do things right, to really make a difference."

James had nodded, pulling her into a hug. "Alright then. We're in this together."

The day Sarah handed in her resignation at Oakwood Bank was both terrifying and exhilarating. David, her manager, had been shocked.

"But Sarah, you're on track for a regional management position," he had sputtered. "Why would you throw that away?"

Sarah had smiled, feeling a weight lift off her shoulders. "Because I want to be a mortgage broker, David, not a salesperson. I want to help people find the right mortgage for them; not just push whatever product the bank wants to sell this month."

As she had walked out of Oakwood Bank for the last time, carrying a box of personal items from her office, Sarah felt a mix of emotions. There was fear, certainly - she was stepping into the unknown. But there was also an overwhelming sense of relief and excitement. For the first time in years, she felt true to herself.

The early days of Sarah's new venture, which she named "Harmony Mortgage Solutions," were filled with boundless optimism. She set up a small office in the spare room of her house, invested in a professional website, and began reaching out to her network to let them know about her new business.

Sarah's vision for Harmony Mortgage Solutions was clear. She wanted to create a brokerage that put clients first, that took the time to understand each individual's unique situation and found the best solution for them, regardless of which lender it came from. She dreamed of building a reputation as the go-to broker for complex cases, the one who could find solutions where others saw only obstacles.

The first few months exceeded even Sarah's optimistic expectations. Her reputation from her time at Oakwood Bank meant that she had a steady stream of clients right from the start. Her personalised approach and willingness to go the extra mile for her clients led to glowing reviews and referrals.

As Sarah successfully closed deal after deal, she felt a deep sense of satisfaction. This was what she had always wanted to do - help people navigate the complex world of mortgages, find the best solutions for their needs, and achieve their dreams of homeownership.

But as the months wore on, the realities of running a business began to set in. The challenges Sarah faced were not the ones she had anticipated, and they tested her resolve in ways she hadn't imagined.

Decision Making: If you have a decision to make that's proving hard, toss a coin. While the coin is in the air, whatever side you are hoping the coin lands on is your decision.

VI. The myth of the Superhero Business Owner

As Sarah stared at her reflection in the bathroom mirror, the memories of those early days of excitement and optimism seemed like a lifetime ago. The reality of running her own company had turned out to be far different from what she had envisioned.

One of the first challenges Sarah encountered was the sheer volume of administrative work involved in running a business. At Oakwood Bank, she had taken for granted the support staff who had handled everything from appointment scheduling to document management. Now, every aspect of the business fell on her shoulders.

Sarah found herself spending hours each day on tasks that had nothing to do with actually helping clients find mortgages. There were invoices to be sent, bills to be paid, compliance paperwork to be filed. The email inbox for Harmony Mortgage Solutions seemed to fill up faster than she could empty it, with every message marked as urgent and demanding her immediate attention.

The feast-or-famine nature of commission-based income was another shock to Sarah's system. At Oakwood Bank, she had been used to a steady payslip & money arriving in her account each month. Now, her income fluctuated wildly. Some months, when several deals closed at once, she would find herself flush with cash. Other months, when deals fell through or were delayed, she would lie awake at night, worrying about how to cover her business expenses and contribute to the household bills.

This financial uncertainty began to take a toll on Sarah's home life. Arguments with James about money became more frequent. "I thought the whole point of this was to have more freedom," he said one night after Sarah had spent yet another weekend working. "But you're working more than ever, and we're living with less financial security."

Sarah had no answer. She knew James was right, but she didn't know how to fix it. The business was growing, but so were the demands on her time and energy.

Perhaps the most challenging aspect of self-employment for Sarah was the isolation. At Oakwood Bank, she had been part of a team. There had always been colleagues to bounce ideas off, to commiserate with after a tough day, to celebrate successes with. Now, she spent her days alone in her home office, with only her computer for company.

The weight of every decision rested solely on Sarah's shoulders. Should she invest in a new CRM system? How should she respond to a negative online review? What should she do about the client who was three months behind on paying their broker fee? There was no one to turn to for advice or support.

As the months turned into years, Sarah found herself working longer and longer hours. She was constantly connected to her phone, responding to client queries at all hours of the day and night. The line between work and personal life blurred until it was almost non-existent.

The toll on Sarah's family life was significant. She found herself missing more and more important moments. There was Lily's school play, where her daughter had looked out into the audience, searching for a mother who wasn't there. There was James' birthday dinner, where Sarah had arrived an hour late, flustered and distracted, her mind still on the difficult client meeting she had just left.

But it was Lily's fifth birthday party that really brought home to Sarah how much she was missing. She had promised Lily she would be there, had even helped plan the party. But on the day, a critical deal had been on the verge of falling apart. Sarah had told herself she just needed to make one quick call to sort things out. One call had turned into a series of frantic negotiations, and before she knew it, the party was over.

When Sarah had finally made it home that evening, the house was quiet. Lily was already in bed. James was in the living room, a half-empty glass of wine in his hand and a look of disappointment on his face.

"She waited for you," James had said quietly. "Kept asking when Mummy was going to arrive. What am I supposed to tell her, Sarah? That Mummy's work is more important than her birthday?"

The words had hit Sarah like a physical blow. She had sunk onto the sofa, burying her face in her hands. "I'm sorry," she had whispered, tears streaming down her face. "I'm so, so sorry."

That night, as Sarah lay awake in bed, the image of Lily's disappointed face haunted her. She had started this business to have more control over her life, to be able to prioritise what really mattered. Instead, she felt more out of control than ever.

VII. The Breaking Point

As Sarah finally stepped into the shower, letting the hot water wash over her tired body, she couldn't shake the feeling that something had to give. The passion that had driven her to start Harmony Mortgage Solutions was still there, buried under layers of stress and exhaustion. She still believed in her vision of a client-focused, ethical company. But the reality of running the business had become overwhelming.

Sarah's days had become a blur of constant activity, each one bleeding into the next. She would wake before dawn, immediately checking her phone for any urgent messages that had come in overnight. Then it was a race against the clock - responding to emails, preparing for client meetings, chasing up lenders for updates on applications, all while trying to keep on top of the ever-growing mountain of administrative tasks.

Lunch was usually a hastily eaten sandwich at her desk, often interrupted by phone calls from anxious clients or demanding estate agents. The afternoon would fly by in a whirlwind of meetings, phone calls, and paperwork. Before she knew it, evening had fallen, and Sarah would realise with a pang of guilt that she had missed dinner with her family once again.

Even when she did manage to tear herself away from work to spend time with James and Lily, Sarah found it increasingly difficult to be truly present. Her mind was constantly preoccupied with work concerns - the deal that was on the brink of falling through, the client who was unhappy with their interest rate, the ever-present worry about where the next lead would come from.

The strain was beginning to show in every aspect of Sarah's life. Her health was suffering - she couldn't remember the last time she had been to the gym or eaten a proper, balanced meal. The constant stress had led to frequent headaches and a persistent knot of tension in her shoulders.

Her relationships were fraying at the edges. James, once her biggest supporter, had become increasingly distant. Their conversations, when they had them, were terse and often ended in arguments. Lily had stopped asking her mother to attend school events or help with homework, having learned through repeated disappointments that Mummy was always "too busy".

Sarah's friends had all but given up on trying to include her in their plans. She had cancelled on them so many times that the invitations had gradually stopped coming. The vibrant social life she had once enjoyed seemed like a distant memory.

As Sarah stepped out of the shower and began to dry herself off, she caught sight of herself in the mirror again. The woman staring back at her was almost unrecognisable from the enthusiastic, optimistic person who had started Harmony Mortgage Solutions three years ago. Her face was drawn and pale, with dark circles under her eyes that no amount of concealer could hide. The spark that had once lit up her eyes when she talked about her work was noticeably absent.

Wrapping herself in a towel, Sarah made her way back to the bedroom. James was still asleep, his back turned towards her side of the bed. Sarah felt a lump form in her throat as she looked at him. When was the last time they had really talked, really connected? She couldn't remember.

As she got dressed for another long day, Sarah's mind wandered to a conversation she had had with a client the previous week. The client, a successful business owner in her fifties, had been refinancing her property portfolio.

"You know, Sarah," the client had said as they were wrapping up their meeting, "you remind me a lot of myself at your age. Driven, passionate about your work, always going the extra mile for your clients."

Sarah had smiled, taking it as a compliment, but the client wasn't finished.

"But let me give you a piece of advice," she had continued, her eyes serious. "Don't make the same mistake I did. Don't sacrifice everything for your business. I spent years working 80-hour weeks, thinking I was building something great. And I did build a successful business, but at what cost? I missed my children growing up. My marriage fell apart. And now, looking back, I realise that no amount of success was worth what I lost."

> *Procrastinating: Procrastination is great as it tells you what you don't want to do or don't enjoy doing. Find someone who enjoys this work and outsource it to them. You are far more valuable focusing on what you enjoy & what you are great at.*

The words had struck a chord with Sarah, but in the rush of her daily routine, she had pushed them to the back of her mind. Now, as she prepared to face another gruelling day, they came back to her with painful clarity.

Sarah made her way downstairs, her footsteps heavy. As she entered the kitchen, she was surprised to find Lily already up, sitting at the table with a bowl of cereal.

"Morning, sweetheart," Sarah said, forcing a smile. "You're up early."

Lily looked up; her expression guarded. "I have a school trip today, remember? You were supposed to sign the permission slip."

Sarah felt her heart sink. She had completely forgotten. "Oh, Lily, I'm so sorry. I'll sign it right now. Where is it?"

"Dad signed it last night," Lily replied, her voice flat. "He said you'd probably be too busy to remember."

The words hit Sarah like a physical blow. She opened her mouth to respond, to apologise, to promise to do better, but no words came out. Lily had already returned her attention to her cereal, clearly not expecting any meaningful response from her mother.

As Sarah moved around the kitchen on autopilot, making herself a coffee she knew she wouldn't have time to drink, she felt as though she was standing on the edge of a precipice. Something had to change, and it had to change soon. But she felt paralysed, unable to see a way forward that didn't involve letting everyone down - her clients, her family, herself.

The sound of her phone ringing cut through the heavy silence of the kitchen. Sarah glanced at the screen and saw it was Tom, a long-standing client she had helped with two previous mortgages. She hesitated for a moment, looking between the phone and Lily, who was studiously avoiding eye contact.

With a heavy heart, Sarah answered the call. "Good morning, Tom. How can I help you?"

As she listened to Tom excitedly explain about an investment property he wanted to move quickly on, Sarah felt a familiar sense of dread wash over her. She should have been on top of this, should have been proactively reaching out to Tom knowing he was in the market for an investment property. Instead, she was on the back foot once again, scrambling to keep up.

"Of course, Tom," she heard herself say. "I'll get right on it. I'll have some options for you by the end of the day."

As she hung up, Sarah realised Lily had left the kitchen without a word. She had missed another opportunity to connect with her daughter, all because of work. The weight of her failure as a mother pressed down on her, making it hard to breathe.

Sarah sank into a chair at the kitchen table, her untouched coffee cooling beside her. She put her head in her hands, feeling utterly overwhelmed. This wasn't the life she had envisioned when she started Harmony Mortgage Solutions. She had wanted to help people, to make a difference, to have control over her own destiny. Instead, she felt more out of control than ever.

The sound of James coming down the stairs jolted Sarah out of her reverie. She quickly sat up, wiping away the tears she hadn't realised were falling. As James entered the kitchen, she could see the concern and frustration warring in his eyes.

"Sarah," he said, his voice gentle but firm. "We need to talk. This can't go on."

Sarah nodded, a lump forming in her throat. "I know," she whispered. "I know it can't."

As James sat down across from her, Sarah felt a glimmer of something she hadn't experienced in a long time - hope. Maybe this was the moment things would start to change. Maybe, just maybe, she could find a way to save her business without sacrificing everything else that mattered.

But as she opened her mouth to speak, her phone buzzed again. A text from her largest client, demanding an urgent call. Sarah looked at James, torn between her responsibilities to her clients and her desperate need to reconnect with her family.

James's face fell, recognising the conflict in Sarah's eyes. "Go," he said, his voice resigned. "We'll talk later."

As Sarah stood up, her heart heavy, she knew she was at a crossroads. Something had to change, and it had to change now. But what? How could she fix this mess she had created?

VIII - Time for change

With shaking hands, Sarah picked up her phone. But instead of responding to the client's text, she found herself scrolling through her contacts. Her finger hovered over a number she had saved months ago but never had the courage to call - a business coach that a colleague had recommended.

Taking a deep breath, Sarah pressed the call button. As the phone began to ring, she felt a mix of anxiety and relief wash over her. She didn't have all the answers, but she was finally ready to admit she needed help.

"Hello, this is Michelle Carter. How can I help you?" a warm, professional voice answered.

Sarah took a deep breath. "Hi Michelle, my name is Sarah Thompson. I'm an independent mortgage broker, and I... I think I need help."

There was a brief pause, and when Michelle spoke again, her voice was filled with understanding.

"Thank you for reaching out, Sarah. It takes courage to ask for help. Can you tell me a bit more about what you're experiencing?"

As Sarah began to explain her situation, the words tumbled out in a rush. She talked about the overwhelming workload, the constant stress, the feeling of being trapped on a hamster wheel with no way off. She described her fears of letting clients down, of missing opportunities, of failing at the business she had poured her heart and soul into. But most of all, she spoke about her family - the missed moments, the strained relationships, the guilt that consumed her.

Michelle listened attentively, occasionally asking clarifying questions. When Sarah finally ran out of words, Michelle's response was both reassuring and galvanising.

"Sarah, what you're experiencing is not uncommon among successful professionals who've transitioned to running their own businesses. The skills that made you an excellent mortgage broker aren't necessarily the same skills needed to run a thriving business. But the good news is, these are skills that can be learned. With the right strategies and support, it's possible to transform your business into one that not only serves your clients well but also supports the life you want to live."

For the first time in months, Sarah felt a glimmer of hope. She wasn't a failure; she was just facing challenges she hadn't been prepared for. And most importantly, she wasn't alone.

As the conversation continued, Sarah and Michelle agreed to meet for an initial consultation. Sarah hung up the phone feeling a mix of emotions - nervousness about the changes ahead, relief at having taken the first step, and excitement about the possibilities that lay before her.

Sarah walked back into the kitchen, where James was still sitting at the table, a look of surprise on his face.

"Who was that?" he asked, clearly not having expected the call to last so long.

Sarah sat down beside him, taking his hand in hers.

"It was a business coach," she said, her voice steady. "James, I'm sorry. For everything. I know things have been awful, and I know it's because of me. But I want you to know - I'm going to fix this. I'm going to make changes. Real changes."

James squeezed her hand, a cautious optimism in his eyes. "I want to believe that, Sarah. I really do."

"I know," Sarah nodded. "And I know I have a lot to prove. But I'm ready to do the work. For our family, for the business, for myself. I don't want to lose what really matters while chasing success."

As they sat there, hands clasped, Sarah felt a shift inside herself. The road ahead would not be easy, but for the first time in a long time, she felt equipped to face the challenges. She was no longer just a mortgage broker struggling to keep up; she was a business owner ready to learn, grow, and build something truly sustainable and fulfilling.

The sun was rising outside, casting a warm glow through the kitchen window. It felt symbolic to Sarah - the dawn of a new chapter in her life and her business. The mortgage broker's dilemma that had brought her to this point was not unique to her. It was a common challenge faced by many in the industry who found themselves trapped between their passion for helping clients and the demands of running a business. But as Sarah was beginning to discover, with the right mindset, tools, and support, it was a dilemma that could be overcome.

As she stood up to get ready for her day, Sarah felt a renewed sense of purpose. The journey of transforming her company was just beginning, and despite the challenges ahead, Sarah felt ready to embrace the change. The days of the overwhelmed, "superhero" mortgage broker was coming to an end. In its place, a new vision was emerging - one of a balanced, thriving business that served clients exceptionally while also supporting the life and goals of its owner.

Sarah turned to James, a small but genuine smile on her face. "I'm going to be late for my first appointment," she said. "But how about we have dinner together tonight? Just the three of us. No phones, no work talk. I want to hear all about Lily's school trip."

James nodded, a matching smile forming on his face. "I'd like that," he said. "We'd both like that very much."

As Sarah gathered her things and prepared to leave, she paused at the front door, taking a deep breath. The day ahead would be challenging, but for the first time in a long time, she felt hopeful about the future. She wasn't just a mortgage broker anymore - she was a business owner on a journey of transformation, ready to face the challenges and seize the opportunities that lay ahead.

With that thought, Sarah stepped out into the morning sunlight, ready to begin the next chapter of her journey from overwhelmed mortgage broker to successful, balanced business owner.

CHAPTER SUMMARY:

In this chapter, we met Sarah, a talented mortgage broker caught in the common industry trap of trying to do everything herself. Through a detailed look at her daily struggles, we explored the myth of the "superhero" mortgage broker and the toll it takes on both personal and professional life. Sarah's breaking point – nearly missing a key opportunity for a valued client – sets the stage for her journey of transformation. Now reflect on your own working patterns and envision a more balanced and efficient approach to running your company.

"Results happen over time, not overnight.
Work hard, be consistent & be patient"

Scan here for the WorkBook

CHAPTER 2: THE FOUR PILLARS OF A SUCCESSFUL COMPANY

Sarah sat in her car, parked outside the office building where she was about to meet Michelle for their first official coaching session. She took a deep breath, feeling a mix of nervousness and excitement. Her mind wandered back to their initial consultation a few weeks ago.

Michelle had surprised Sarah from the very beginning. Unlike other coaches Sarah had spoken to, who had launched into sales pitches about their services, Michelle had started their conversation by emphasising the importance of finding the right coach-client fit.

"Sarah," Michelle had said, her voice warm but professional, "before we go any further, I want you to understand something. The relationship between a coach and a client is crucial to the success of the coaching process. It's not just about the coach's qualifications or methods – it's about creating a bond of trust and understanding."

Sarah had nodded, intrigued by this approach.

Michelle continued, "That's why I always encourage potential clients to meet with several coaches before making a decision. It's more important to me that you find the coach that's right for you, rather than feeling pressured to work with me specifically."

This statement had taken Sarah aback. In her experience, most professionals were eager to secure new clients, not encourage them to shop around. Michelle's confidence and genuine concern for Sarah's best interests were refreshing.

"Really?" Sarah had asked. "You don't mind if I meet with other coaches?"

Michelle had smiled. "Not at all. In fact, I insist on it. Coaching is an investment in yourself and your business. You need to feel completely comfortable with your coach, to trust them implicitly. That kind of relationship can't be forced – it has to feel right."

Over the next two weeks, Sarah had taken Michelle's advice and met with three other business coaches. Each had their own strengths and impressive credentials. But none of them had made Sarah feel as at ease and understood as Michelle had.

There was something about Michelle's blend of professionalism and warmth, her obvious expertise combined with a genuine interest in Sarah as a person, not just a potential client. Sarah had found herself opening up to Michelle in a way she hadn't with the others, sharing not just her business challenges but her hopes and fears for the future.

When Sarah had called Michelle to say she wanted to work with her, Michelle's response had been characteristically thoughtful.

"I'm honoured that you've chosen to work with me, Sarah," she had said. "But before we make it official, I want you to take one more day to reflect. Make sure this feels right to you. Remember, for this process to work, you need to be fully committed and comfortable."

That final demonstration of putting Sarah's needs first had cemented her decision. She knew she had found not just a coach, but a partner in her journey to transform her business.

Now, as Sarah stepped out of her car and walked towards the office building, she felt a sense of calm certainty. Yes, she was about to embark on a challenging journey of change and growth. But she knew she had chosen the right guide for that journey.

Sarah knocked on Michelle's office door, and as she heard the warm "Come in!" from inside, she felt ready to face whatever lay ahead. It was time to begin the transformation of her company, and she couldn't imagine a better person to help her do it than Michelle.

As she stepped into Michelle's office, Sarah was greeted with a warm smile. "Welcome back, Sarah. How have you been since our last meeting?"

Sarah settled into the comfortable chair across from Michelle. "Honestly? A bit overwhelmed, but also... hopeful. I've been thinking a lot about what we discussed last time. I can see areas where I need to improve, but I'm not sure where to start."

Michelle nodded understandingly. "That's perfectly normal, Sarah. Today, we're going to dive deeper into a framework that I believe will help bring clarity and structure to your business. We call it the Four Pillars of a Successful Company."

Sarah leaned forward, intrigued. "Four Pillars? What do you mean?"

The Four Main Pillars To Any Successful Business

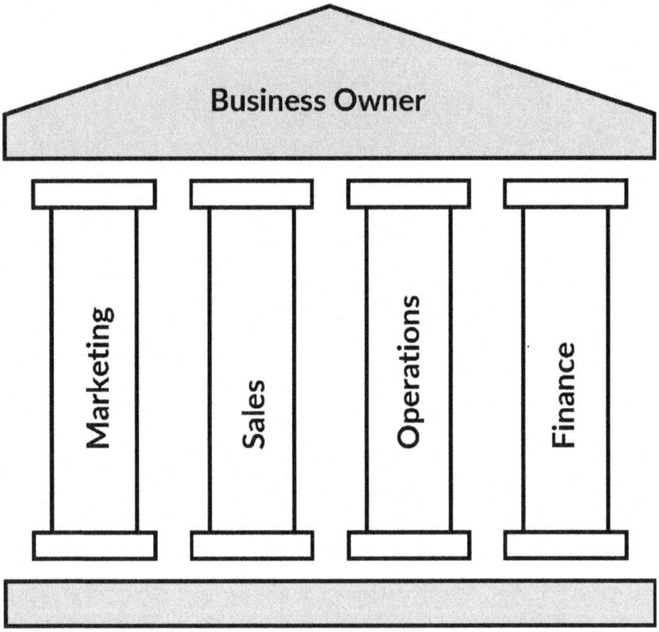

Michelle stood and walked to the whiteboard, where she drew four vertical lines. "Let's start by introducing what each pillar represents."

1. Marketing: Attracting Your Ideal Clients
2. Sales: Converting Leads into Loyal Customers
3. Operations: Streamlining Your Brokerage
4. Finance: Managing the Lifeblood of Your Business

"Think of your brokerage as a table," Michelle explained, sketching a quick table supported by the four pillars. "Each of these pillars is a leg. If one is weak or missing, what happens?"

Sarah pictured a wobbly table, ready to collapse at any moment. It was an uncomfortable parallel to how her business felt right now. "It becomes unstable," she replied. "Everything becomes harder to manage."

"Exactly," Michelle confirmed. "A successful company needs all four pillars to be strong and in balance. When they are, your business becomes stable, efficient, and primed for growth. I've seen this simple model successfully work for every type of company".

The Marketing Pillar: Attracting Your Ideal Clients

Michelle began with the first pillar. "Marketing is about more than just getting your name out there. It's about attracting the right clients - those who align with your expertise and values."

Sarah nodded slowly. "I've always struggled with marketing. It feels like I'm shouting into the void, hoping someone will hear."

Michelle smiled empathetically. "That's a common feeling. Let's break it down. Effective marketing involves several key components:

1. **Defining Your Unique Value Proposition (UVP):** What makes you different from other brokers? Why should a potential client choose you?
2. **Identifying Your Ideal Client:** Who can you serve best? What are their needs, fears, and aspirations?
3. **Creating a Consistent Brand Message:** This goes beyond a logo. It's about the personality and values you project across all touchpoints.
4. **Developing a Multi-Channel Marketing Strategy:** This might include digital marketing, networking, referral partnerships, and community involvement.
5. **Content Marketing:** Sharing your expertise through blogs, videos, or social media to position yourself as a trusted advisor.
6. **Measuring and Analysing Results:** Using data to understand what's working and what isn't."

Sarah felt a mix of excitement and apprehension. "That sounds comprehensive, but also... a lot of work. How do I manage all of that while still running my business?"

Michelle nodded. "It can feel overwhelming at first. The key is to start small and build gradually. Let's take a moment to assess where you are now with your marketing efforts."

They spent the next few minutes discussing Sarah's current marketing activities. It became clear that while Sarah had a website and occasionally attended networking events, her approach was inconsistent and largely reactive.

"Okay," Michelle said, making notes. "We've identified that marketing is an area that needs significant improvement. But don't worry - this is an opportunity. By developing a strategic marketing approach, you can attract more of your ideal clients and set the foundation for growth in other areas of your business."

The Sales Pillar: Converting Leads into Loyal Customers

Moving on to the second pillar, Michelle explained, "Sales in the mortgage industry isn't about pushing products. It's about guiding clients to the right solution for their needs. Your role is part educator, part problem-solver, and part trusted advisor."

Sarah nodded, feeling more confident. "This is where I feel strongest. I'm good at explaining complex mortgage concepts to clients and finding solutions for them."

"That's excellent, Sarah," Michelle encouraged. "Let's build on that strength. A robust sales process for a mortgage broker typically includes:

1. A structured sales funnel: From initial inquiry to post-completion care.
2. Consultative selling techniques: Asking the right questions to uncover clients' true needs and goals.
3. Effective communication skills: Clearly explaining complex concepts and actively listening to clients.
4. Objection handling: Anticipating and addressing common concerns.
5. Follow-up systems: Ensuring no lead falls through the cracks.
6. Technology integration: Using CRM systems to manage client relationships effectively."

Sarah's mind was racing with ideas. "I can see how having a more structured approach could help me convert more leads and provide better service to my clients."

Michelle nodded approvingly. "Exactly. And the beauty of it is that a well-designed sales process supports your natural strengths rather than constraining them."

The Operations Pillar: Streamlining Your Business

"Now," Michelle continued, "let's talk about operations. This is often the unsung hero of successful businesses. It's about creating systems and processes that allow your business to run smoothly and scale effectively."

Sarah's expression turned sheepish. "I have to admit, this is probably my weakest area. Everything feels a bit chaotic most of the time."

Michelle reassured her, "That's not uncommon, especially for brokers who've grown their business organically. But strong operations can transform your daily work life and significantly boost your efficiency. Key aspects of operations for any company include:

1. Workflow optimisation: Mapping out and refining your core processes.
2. Document management: Implementing systems for organise and retrieving client documents efficiently.
3. Technology integration: Choosing and implementing the right programmes that support your business processes.
4. Team management: As you grow, having clear roles, responsibilities, and communication channels. Also, how to recruit & maintain the right staff for your business.
5. Compliance management: Ensuring you have systems in place to meet regulatory requirements consistently.
6. Continuous improvement: Regularly reviewing and refining your processes."

Sarah looked thoughtful. "I can see how improving my operations could free up a lot of time and reduce stress. But where do I start?"

"A good place to start is by mapping out your current processes," Michelle suggested. "Once you can see your workflows clearly, it becomes much easier to identify bottlenecks and areas for improvement."

The Finance Pillar: Managing the Lifeblood of Your Business

"Finally," Michelle said, moving to the last pillar, "let's talk about finance. This isn't just about keeping the books balanced. It's about using financial data to make informed decisions and drive your business forward."

Sarah shifted uncomfortably in her seat. "I have to confess; finance has always been my blind spot. I know I make money, but beyond that, it's all a bit foggy."

Michelle nodded understandingly. "You're not alone in that. Many business owners struggle with financial management. But as a mortgage broker, you have a head start in understanding financial principles. We just need to apply those skills to your own business. Key aspects of financial management for any company include:

1. Budgeting and forecasting: Planning for future expenses and revenue.
2. Cash flow management: Ensuring you always have enough cash to meet your obligations.
3. Profitability analysis: Analyse which activities are most profitable for your business.
4. Financial reporting: Regular review of key financial statements.
5. Tax planning: Staying compliant and minimising your tax burden legally.
6. Investment decisions: Making informed choices about reinvesting in your business."

Sarah nodded slowly, beginning to see the importance of this pillar. "I can see how having a clearer financial picture could help me make better decisions about everything else in my business."

"Exactly," Michelle agreed. "Finance is the scoreboard of your business. It tells you how well you're doing in all other areas."

The Interconnectedness of the Four Pillars

Michelle stood back from the whiteboard, which was now covered in notes about each pillar. "Now, here's where it gets really interesting. These pillars don't exist in isolation. They're deeply interconnected."

Sarah leaned forward, intrigued. "What do you mean?"

"Well," Michelle explained, drawing arrows between the pillars, "think about it this way:

- Your marketing efforts directly impact your sales pipeline.
- Your sales process influences how you need to structure your operations.
- Your operational efficiency affects your financial performance.
- Your financial resources determine what you can invest in marketing and other areas of the business.

It's a virtuous cycle when all pillars are strong and working together."

Sarah's eyes widened as she began to see the bigger picture. "So, by strengthening one pillar, I'm actually supporting the others as well?"

"Exactly!" Michelle beamed. "That's why this approach is so powerful. It creates a holistic view of your business, allowing you to make strategic decisions that benefit the entire operation. Also, by understanding that your workflow is Marketing then sales then operations then finance, it's easy to pinpoint problems in the company as you always work on the problem area plus the preceding area".

- Not enough sales then are you maximising the leads you are getting (Sales) or are you not producing enough of the right quality leads (Marketing)
- Team not hitting target then are they running efficiently (Operations) or are they not being passed sufficient opportunities (Sales)

- Marketing not producing results. Is the marketing team understanding expectations (Marketing) or do they not have sufficient budget for success (Finance)

Always look at the problem area then start working back around that virtuous circle.

Workflow through your company

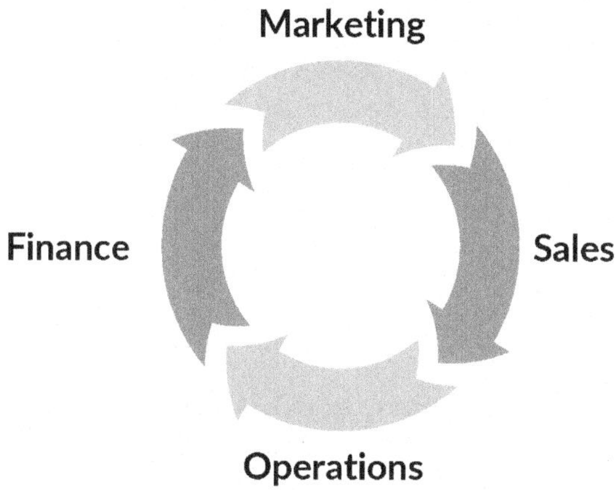

Workflow when problem solving

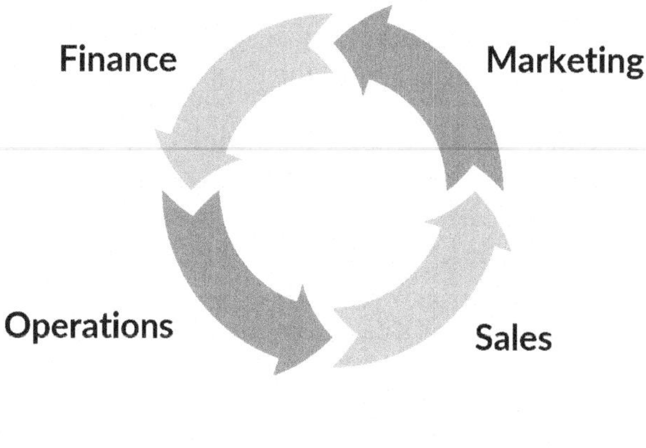

Start with the problem area and work backwards

Assessing Your Current State

Michelle pulled out a worksheet and handed it to Sarah. "Now, let's do a quick assessment of where your business stands in each of these areas. This will give us a starting point for improvement."

Sarah looked at the worksheet, which asked her to rate her business from 1 to 10 in each pillar.

"Be honest with yourself," Michelle encouraged. "This isn't about judgment. It's about identifying opportunities for growth."

Sarah took a deep breath and began to fill out the worksheet:

- Marketing: 3
- Sales: 7
- Operations: 2
- Finance: 2

As she looked at her ratings, Sarah felt a mix of disappointment and motivation. "Wow, seeing it laid out like this really drives home where I need to improve."

Michelle nodded encouragingly. "This is a great first step, Sarah. Awareness is the beginning of change. Now, let's dig a little deeper into each area."

They spent the next hour discussing the specific strengths and challenges Sarah faced in each pillar. Michelle asked probing questions, helping Sarah articulate the reasons behind her ratings.

For marketing, Sarah realised that while she had a strong reputation for customer service, she lacked a systematic approach to attracting new clients. Her sales rating was higher due to her natural ability to connect with clients, but she acknowledged that her process was largely intuitive rather than structured & definitely wouldn't be scalable when growth started to happen.

Operations emerged as a significant pain point, with Sarah describing the constant feeling of being overwhelmed by administrative tasks. And in finance, she admitted to a "head in the sand" approach, managing primarily by her bank balance rather than through proper financial planning and analysis.

Visioning Exercise

"Now that we have a clear picture of where you are," Michelle said, "let's talk about where you want to be. I want you to imagine your business operating at a '10' in each of these areas. What would that look like?"

Sarah closed her eyes, allowing herself to envision her ideal brokerage. She described a business with a strong brand presence, a steady stream of ideal clients, a smooth and efficient sales process, streamlined operations that ran like clockwork, and clear financial insights that guided every business decision.

As she opened her eyes, Sarah felt a surge of excitement. "Is that really possible?" she asked, a hint of doubt in her voice.

Michelle smiled warmly. "Absolutely. It won't happen overnight, but with consistent effort and the right strategies, you can transform your business in each of these areas."

Action Planning

"Now," Michelle continued, "based on what we've discussed, what's one concrete action you can take in the next week to start improving your weakest pillar?"

Sarah thought for a moment. "Well, operations are clearly my weakest area. I think... I could start by creating a detailed log of how I spend my time each day. That would help me identify where I'm losing time and what tasks are taking up most of my day."

"Excellent choice," Michelle approved. "Time tracking is a great first step in improving operational efficiency. Let's set a specific goal around that."

Together, they formulated a plan for Sarah to track her time in detail for the next week, using a simple app on her phone to log her activities.

The Power of Reflection

As their session neared its end, Michelle posed one final question. "Sarah, how do you think improving your weakest pillar - operations in this case - might positively impact the other pillars of your business?"

Sarah pondered this for a moment. "Well, if I can streamline my operations, I'd have more time to focus on marketing and developing my sales process. And I suppose with better systems in place, it would be easier to track my finances and make informed decisions."

Michelle nodded approvingly. "Exactly. That's the power of the Four Pillars approach. Improvements in one area create a ripple effect, benefiting your entire business."

Time Audit: A Deeper Dive into Operations

Given that operations emerged as Sarah's weakest pillar, Michelle suggested a more in-depth exercise to gain clarity in this area.

"For the next five working days," Michelle explained, "I want you to set an hourly alarm on your phone. Each time the alarm sounds, record what tasks you had completed over the past hour. This will give us a detailed picture of how you're spending your time and help identify any inefficiencies in your current working style. I'm not going to lie, this will seem an arduous process and you'll want to give up on it by day three but I must insist you stick with it as you'll be truly shocked by the outcome".

Sarah nodded, already feeling a bit apprehensive about what this exercise might reveal. "Okay, I can do that. But what exactly should I be looking for?"

Michelle smiled reassuringly. "Don't worry about analysing it as you go. Just focus on recording your activities as accurately as possible. After the five days, we'll review the data together and look for patterns. We'll be able to identify:

1. Time sinks: Activities that are taking up a disproportionate amount of your time.
2. Inefficiencies: Processes that could be streamlined or automated.
3. Value-add vs. non-value-add activities: Distinguishing between tasks that directly contribute to your business growth and those that don't.
4. Peak productivity times: Identifying when you're most efficient and effective.

This information will be invaluable in redesigning your workflows and improving your overall operational efficiency."

Homework: Envisioning Your Ideal Working Day

As a final exercise, Michelle asked Sarah to complete one more task before their next meeting.

"After you've completed the time audit," Michelle instructed, "I want you to write a brief description of your ideal working day as a mortgage broker. How would you spend your time if your business was operating at peak efficiency? What tasks would you be focusing on? How would it feel?"

Sarah nodded, already beginning to imagine the possibilities.

Michelle continued, "Then, I want you to compare this vision to your current reality as revealed by the time audit. This comparison will help us identify the gaps between where you are and where you want to be, giving us clear targets for improvement."

Wrapping Up

As their session came to a close, Sarah felt a mix of emotions - excitement about the possibilities ahead, nervousness about the work involved, but overall, a sense of hope and direction that had been missing for a long time.

Michelle sensed Sarah's mood. "Remember, Sarah, this is a journey. We're not going to transform your business overnight. But by focusing on these Four Pillars and consistently working to strengthen each one, you'll see remarkable changes over time."

Sarah nodded, feeling more determined than ever. "Thank you, Michelle. This has been eye-opening. I'm looking forward to diving into these exercises and seeing where this takes me."

As Sarah left the office, her mind was already buzzing with ideas. The Four Pillars framework had given her a new way of looking at her business, a clear structure for improvement, and a roadmap for growth. She knew the journey ahead would be challenging, but for the first time in a long while, she felt truly excited about the future of her company.

CHAPTER 2 SUMMARY: THE FOUR PILLARS OF A SUCCESSFUL COMPANY

In this chapter, we introduced the concept of the Four Pillars of a successful company: Marketing, Sales, Operations, and Finance. Through Sarah's coaching session with Michelle, we explored the importance of each pillar and the consequences of neglecting any one of them.

Key takeaways:

1. Marketing: Focuses on attracting the right clients through a clear value proposition, targeted strategies, and consistent branding.
2. Sales: Emphasizes a structured, consultative approach to guiding clients towards the right mortgage solutions.
3. Operations: Highlights the importance of efficient workflows, robust CRM systems, and effective document management.
4. Finance: Stresses the need for clear financial management and planning in the brokerage business.

The chapter underscored the interconnectedness of these areas and set the stage for a deeper dive into each pillar

Scan here for the WorkBook

WORKSHEET: ASSESSING YOUR COMPANY'S FOUR PILLARS

Part 1: Self-Assessment

Rate your company on each of the four pillars from 1 to 10 (1 being weakest, 10 being strongest):

- Marketing: ______________________
- Sales: ______________________
- Operations: ______________________
- Finance: ______________________

Part 2: Strengths and Weaknesses

Identify your strongest and weakest pillars based on your ratings above.

Strongest Pillar: ______________________

List three specific reasons why you excel in this area:

1. ______________________
2. ______________________
3. ______________________

Weakest Pillar: ______________________

List three specific challenges you face in this area:

1. ______________________
2. ______________________
3. ______________________

Part 3: Vision Exercise

For each pillar, write a brief description of what a "10 out of 10" would look like in your brokerage:

Marketing (10/10):

Sales (10/10):

Operations (10/10):

Finance (10/10):

Part 4: Action Planning

Based on your self-assessment and vision exercise, identify one concrete action you can take in the next week to improve your weakest pillar:

Action: ______________________________

Deadline: ______________________________

Part 5: Reflection

How might improving your weakest pillar positively impact the other pillars of your business?

____

____

____

____

Part 6: Time Audit

For the next five working days, set an hourly alarm on your phone. Each time the alarm sounds, record what tasks you had completed over the past hour. Identify time sinks and inefficiencies in your current working style.

Reflection: With this time log completed, note which tasks need to be performed by a qualified person & which tasks could be performed by an administrator or less qualified person.

Vision Setting: Write a brief description of your ideal working day. How does it differ from your current reality?

Remember, a successful business requires strength in all four pillars and the time to address them. Use this worksheet as a starting point to identify areas for improvement and set goals for your business growth.

CHAPTER 3:
MARKETING - ATTRACTING YOUR IDEAL CLIENTS

Marketing Momentum: Your first marketing idea is rarely your best - it's just the most obvious. Write down your first five ideas, then force yourself to generate five more. The unique angles usually emerge when you push past the obvious.

Sarah stared at the blank page, pen in hand. "Write down what makes you unique," her coach had said. But all Sarah could think was that she helped people get mortgages - just like every other broker out there.

At their previous meeting, Michelle had asked Sarah who she thought her ideal client was. "It's anyone with a mortgage" Sarah had responded.

"Potentially, yes Sarah. But how do you send a marketing message with the ability to resonate with everybody that has a mortgage, which equates to at least two thirds of homeowners?"

"I don't understand" Sarah replied.

Michelle smiled, "think about who you get the greatest pleasure helping. Why do you get such pleasure from this group of people and what makes your work so valuable to them? Once you know that you know the exact message you need to send which will really resonate with your chosen group".

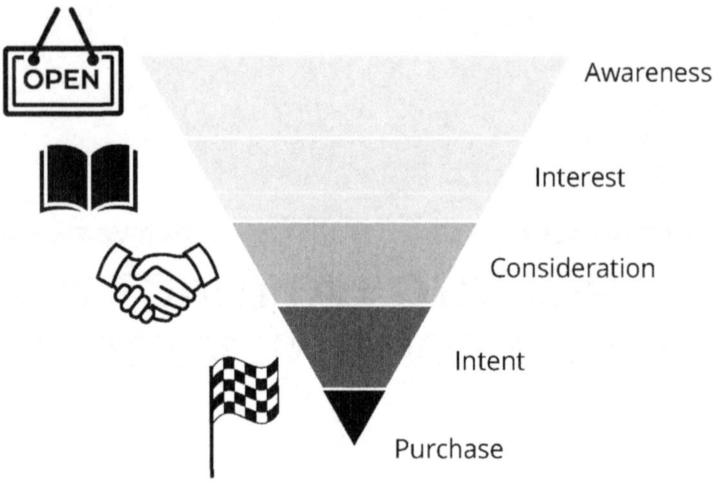

The luxury of time had let this comment take root in Sarah's head. She leaned back in her chair & closed her eyes. Suddenly, faces began to float through her mind - clients she had helped over the years. There was Mrs. Johnson, an elderly widow who had thanked Sarah profusely for her patience in explaining every step of the refinancing process. Then the young couple, first-time buyers with unconventional income sources, who had been turned down by three banks before Sarah found them a suitable lender.

Opening her eyes, Sarah began to write: "I don't just arrange mortgages. I guide my clients through one of the biggest financial decisions of their lives, with patience, clarity, and creative problem-solving."

As the words flowed onto the page, Sarah felt a shift. This wasn't just a marketing exercise anymore. It was the beginning of her brand, the core of her value proposition. She wasn't just another mortgage broker. She was a financial guide, a problem-solver, a patient educator.

With renewed energy, Sarah turned to her computer and pulled up her neglected website. The generic stock photos and vague promises of "great rates" suddenly seemed woefully inadequate.

She began to sketch out ideas for client stories, educational content, and a clear articulation of her unique approach.

For the first time, Sarah felt excited about marketing. She wasn't just promoting a service; she was sharing her passion for helping people achieve their dreams of homeownership. And in doing so, she was finally differentiating herself in a crowded market.

The Marketing Mindset Shift

As Sarah delved deeper into her marketing journey, she realised that effective marketing for a mortgage broker wasn't just about promoting products or rates. It was about building relationships, establishing trust, and demonstrating expertise. This was the part of the mortgage process that most appealed to Sarah.

She thought back to her conversation with Michelle about the importance of a client-centric approach.

"Your clients don't just want a mortgage, in fact that's the last thing they want," Michelle had said. "What they actually want is a home, financial security & a better future. If they could achieve that without the need for a mortgage it would certainly be their preferred option. Your marketing should speak to those deeper desires and show how you can help them achieve their goals."

With this in mind, Sarah began to reframe her entire approach to marketing. Instead of focusing solely on mortgage products, she started thinking about the life events that typically trigger a need for her services:

1. First-time buyers taking their first step onto the property ladder
2. Growing families looking to upsize
3. Professionals relocating for work
4. Couples going through divorce and needing to refinance
5. Retirees considering equity release options

Each of these life stages came with its own set of hopes, fears, and challenges. Sarah realised that if she could address these in her marketing, she'd be much more likely to connect with potential clients on a meaningful level.

Sarah jotted down some ideas:

- For first-time buyers: "From rental to ownership: Navigate the exciting journey to your first home with confidence."
- For growing families: "Room to grow: Find the perfect mortgage to upsize your home as your family expands."
- For relocating professionals: "New job, new home: Seamless mortgage solutions for your career move."
- For divorcing couples: "Financial fresh start: Compassionate refinancing guidance during life transitions."
- For retirees: "Unlock your property's potential: Expert advice on equity release for a comfortable retirement."

As she looked at these ideas, Sarah felt a sense of excitement. This wasn't just about selling mortgages; it was about connecting with people at crucial moments in their lives and helping them achieve their goals.

Short-Term vs Long-Term Marketing Strategies

During their next session, Michelle introduced Sarah to the concept of balancing short-term and long-term marketing strategies.

"Think of your marketing efforts like tending a garden, Sarah," Michelle explained. "Some strategies are like annuals - they bloom quickly but need constant replanting. Others are like perennials - they take longer to establish but provide beauty year after year."

Sarah leaned forward, intrigued. "So, what would be examples of each in the mortgage industry?"

Michelle smiled, pleased at Sarah's engagement. "Let's break it down."

Short-Term Strategies:

1. **Pay-Per-Click (PPC) Advertising:**

   "This is like planting annuals," Michelle said. "You can see results quickly, but it requires ongoing investment."

   Sarah nodded, thinking aloud. "So, I could set up Google Ads campaigns targeting specific keywords like 'first-time buyer mortgage' or 'remortgage deals' in Manchester?"

   "Exactly," Michelle confirmed. "It's possible to appear at the top of search results immediately, but you'd pay for each click. Also, Google will still want to see that you're an authority on each term you're bidding for so you will need content around that subject on your website."

   Sarah made a note to research popular mortgage-related keywords in her area. She thought about creating separate ad campaigns for different client segments: first-time buyers, remortgages, buy-to-let investors, and those with complex income situations.

2. **Social Media Advertising:**

   "Similarly," Michelle continued, "you could create targeted Facebook and Instagram ads showcasing your services to specific demographics in your local area."

   Sarah's mind raced with possibilities. "I could create ads targeting newlyweds in Manchester about first-time buyer mortgages, or ads about equity release for retirees in Cheshire."

   She imagined a carousel ad on Facebook, each slide addressing a different life stage and the corresponding mortgage needs. The first slide might show a young couple with the text

"Ready to buy your first home?", while another could feature a retired couple with "Considering equity release?"

Michelle saw the excitement in Sarah's eyes and cautioned her "Sarah, this is a marathon, not a sprint. The key to social media marketing is three words – Consistent, persistent and relevant. Once you start this social media journey you must be posting as regularly as possible but a minimum of three times each week and the content must be engaging not just sales biased. Remember the word "social" is in social media".

3. **Limited-Time Offers:**

   "These create a sense of urgency," Michelle explained. "For example, you could offer a free consultation and personalised mortgage comparison report for inquiries made within a specific timeframe."

   Sarah thought about how she could implement this. "Maybe I could run a 'Spring Home Buying Consultation' offer, providing a free 30-minute consultation and personalised report for anyone who books in April. It could coincide with the typically busy spring property market."

4. **Local Event Sponsorship:**

   "This gives you immediate exposure to a relevant audience," Michelle said. "You could sponsor a local property auction or a first-time buyer seminar."

   Sarah remembered a local property investment group that held monthly meetings. "I could sponsor one of their events," she mused. "I could even offer to give a short presentation on mortgage options for investors."

Sarah jotted down these ideas, already thinking about how she could implement them. She could see how these strategies could bring quick results, helping her to generate leads and build momentum in her business.

Long-Term Strategies:

1. **Content Marketing:**

> *"Content marketing is like a first date. If you only talk about yourself, there won't be a second one."*
> **– David Beebe**

"This is a key perennial strategy," Michelle emphasised. "By consistently producing valuable content, you establish yourself as an expert and build trust over time."

Sarah thought about her neglected blog.

"So, I should be regularly writing articles about mortgage-related topics?"

"Exactly," Michelle nodded. "But don't limit yourself to just written content. Consider starting a YouTube channel or a podcast. You could create a series called 'Understanding the Property Market' or 'How to Improve Your Mortgage Affordability'."

Sarah's mind whirled with ideas. She could create a weekly video series called "Mortgage Myths Busted", addressing common misconceptions about mortgages. Or a podcast interviewing local property experts, from estate agents to surveyors, providing a comprehensive guide to the property buying process.

2. **Search Engine Optimisation (SEO):**

"This goes hand-in-hand with content marketing," Michelle explained. "By optimising your website for key search terms, you can improve your organic search rankings over time."

Sarah made a note to research more about SEO.

"So, I should be creating content around terms people are searching for, like 'how to get a mortgage with bad credit' or 'best buy-to-let mortgages in Manchester'?"

"Precisely," Michelle smiled. "And don't forget location-specific content. 'Guide to Buying Property in Manchester' or 'London First-Time Buyer Schemes Explained' could be great for attracting local clients."

Sarah realised she could create a series of in-depth guides for different areas in her region, each optimised for local search terms. This could help her attract clients from specific neighbourhoods and demonstrate her local market knowledge.

3. **Referral Network Building:**

   "This is about cultivating relationships that will yield referrals over time," Michelle said. "Focus on building strong connections with estate agents, solicitors, and financial advisors."

   Sarah thought about the professionals she already knew in these fields. She could start by reaching out to them, perhaps offering to create co-branded content or host joint webinars. Over time, she could expand this network, becoming the go-to mortgage expert for other property professionals in her area.

4. **Brand Building:**

"A brand is the set of expectations, memories, stories and relationships that, taken together, account for a consumer's decision to choose one product or service over another."
– Seth Godin

   "This is the slow but steady work of consistently delivering exceptional service and encouraging satisfied clients to leave reviews," Michelle explained. "Over time, you'll build a reputation as the go-to mortgage broker in your area."

Michelle added, "think of when clients reach a milestone that delivers satisfaction. Each of these points can be used as prompts for requests for testimonials or referrals. You don't have to wait to the end of the sales process to make your request".

Sarah realised she needed a systematic approach to collecting and showcasing client testimonials. She could create a follow-up process, reaching out to clients after their mortgage completion to ask for feedback and reviews. These could then be featured prominently on her website and social media channels.

5. **Email Marketing:**

   "Build an email list of prospects and past clients," Michelle advised. "Send regular, valuable content to stay top-of-mind for when they need mortgage services. The key here is to keep whatever you are sending both informative and relevant"

   Sarah envisioned a monthly newsletter, featuring market updates, mortgage tips, and perhaps a client success story. For past clients, she could include reminders about remortgaging opportunities or information about using additional borrowing for home improvements.

Sarah felt a bit overwhelmed by all the options, but also excited about the possibilities. "How do I balance these short-term and long-term strategies?" she asked.

Michelle smiled. "That's the art of it, Sarah. You need to find the right mix for your business. Short-term strategies can bring quick results, which can be motivating and provide cash flow. But don't neglect the long-term strategies - they're what will build your brand and create sustainable success."

Sarah nodded, already starting to formulate a plan in her mind. She could see how combining these strategies could help her reach a wider range of potential clients and build a stronger, more resilient business.

"I could start with some PPC advertising to generate immediate leads," Sarah thought aloud. "But alongside that, I'll commit to creating regular content for my blog and social media. Maybe I could aim for one in-depth article and two short video tips each week?"

Michelle nodded approvingly. "That sounds like a good balance. Remember, consistency is key with the long-term strategies. It's better to commit to a

Sarah thought about how she could showcase this UVP across her marketing channels:

- On her website homepage: A prominent headline stating "Complex Income? We've Got You Covered" followed by brief explanations of how she helps different types of non-standard borrowers.
- In her social media bios:"Manchester's go-to mortgage broker for self-employed, contractors, and complex income cases."
- Through case studies: Detailed stories of how she'd helped clients with unique financial situations secure mortgages.
- In her email signature: A brief tagline encapsulating her UVP, linking to a dedicated landing page on her website.

Sarah realised that by consistently communicating this unique value proposition, she could attract more of her ideal clients - those with complex needs who would truly benefit from her expertise and patient approach.

Creating a Consistent Brand Message

With her UVP in place, Sarah turned her attention to creating a consistent brand message across all her marketing channels. She realised that her brand wasn't just about a logo or colour scheme - it was about the personality and values she wanted to project.

She defined her brand attributes:

- Professional yet approachable
- Knowledgeable but not condescending
- Patient and detail-oriented
- Innovative in finding solutions
- Trustworthy and transparent

These attributes would guide everything from the tone of her website copy to the way she interacted with clients on social media.

Sarah spent time thinking about how these attributes could be reflected in her communications:

1. Professional yet approachable: "I'll use a friendly, conversational tone in my writing, but always maintain professionalism. No industry jargon without clear explanations." Sarah imagined rewriting her website's 'About' page. Instead of a dry list of qualifications, she could share her journey into mortgage broking, perhaps touching on a personal experience that drove her passion for helping others achieve homeownership.
2. Knowledgeable but not condescending: "I'll share complex information in easily digestible formats, like infographics or short video explainers." She thought about creating a series of "Mortgage Basics" videos, each under two minutes long, explaining key concepts like LTV ratios or the difference between fixed and variable rates.
3. Patient and detail-oriented: "I'll create comprehensive guides for different mortgage scenarios, showing that I'm willing to take the time to explain things thoroughly." Sarah envisioned a downloadable "First-Time Buyer's Roadmap", outlining every step from saving for a deposit to completing on a property, with her guidance available at each stage. She would create a video version of all her educational material to ensure she had a learning format to suit all.

4. Innovative in finding solutions: "I'll share case studies of how I've helped clients with particularly challenging situations." She could create a monthly "Problem Solved" feature on her blog, anonymising details but showcasing how she'd overcome complex financial obstacles for her clients.
5. Trustworthy and transparent: "I'll be upfront about my fees and the mortgage process, and I'll share client testimonials prominently." Sarah decided to create a "How I Work" page on her website, clearly outlining her process, fees, and what clients could expect when working with her. She'd also create a video testimonial section, featuring real clients sharing their experiences.

Sarah created a brand style guide to ensure consistency across all her marketing materials. This included guidelines on:

- Logo usage: How and where to use her logo, including minimum sizes and clear space requirements.
- Colour palette: A primary colour (a calming blue, representing trust and professionalism) and secondary colours (warm orange for energy and approachability, and green for growth and financial health).
- Typography: A clean, modern sans-serif font for headings to convey professionalism, paired with a readable serif font for body text to add a touch of warmth and tradition.
- Tone of voice: Friendly and conversational, but always professional. Use of "you" and "we" to create a sense of partnership with clients.
- Image style: Real, authentic images of local Manchester neighbourhoods and people, avoiding clichéd stock photos.

She realised that consistency in these elements would help build recognition and trust with her audience over time. Every touchpoint, from her business card to her email newsletter, would reinforce her brand attributes and value proposition.

Compliance Considerations: GDPR and FCA Regulations

As Sarah began to plan her marketing strategies, she knew she needed to ensure compliance with both GDPR and FCA regulations. She scheduled a meeting with a compliance consultant to review her plans.

The consultant emphasised several key points:

1. **Consent**: Under GDPR, Sarah needed explicit consent from individuals before sending marketing communications. This meant creating clear opt-in mechanisms on her website and other lead generation tools. Sarah decided to implement a double opt-in process for her email newsletter. When someone signed up, they'd receive an email asking them to confirm their subscription. This would ensure that only those genuinely interested in her content would be added to her list.
2. **Data Protection**: Sarah needed to ensure that any personal data collected for marketing purposes was stored securely and used only for the purposes for which it was collected. She made a note to review her data storage practices, ensuring all client information was encrypted and access was restricted to only those who needed it. She also decided to conduct regular data audits to ensure she wasn't holding onto information longer than necessary.
3. **Right to be Forgotten**: Sarah needed to have processes in place to remove individuals from her marketing lists if they requested it. She created a clear unsubscribe process for her email marketing and drafted a policy for handling data deletion requests promptly and efficiently.
4. **Financial Promotions**: The FCA had strict rules about financial promotions. Any marketing material that promoted specific mortgage products needed to be fair, clear, and not misleading. Risk warnings needed to be included where appropriate. Sarah decided to create a checklist for all her marketing materials, ensuring each piece included necessary

disclaimers and risk warnings. She also committed to having all financial promotions reviewed by a compliance expert before publication.

5. **Advice vs. Information**: Sarah needed to be careful to distinguish between providing general information (which could be done in marketing materials) and giving advice (which required a full fact-find and suitability assessment). In her content marketing, Sarah made sure to include clear disclaimers that the information provided was for general purposes only and did not constitute financial advice. She created a standard footer for all blog posts and videos explaining this.
6. **Record Keeping**: Both GDPR and FCA regulations required careful record-keeping. Sarah needed to document her marketing activities, including how consent was obtained and how data was used. She implemented a system to log all marketing activities, including dates of campaigns, target audiences, and any responses or opt-outs received.

Sarah realised that compliance wasn't just a box-ticking exercise - it was about building trust with her clients and protecting their interests. She decided to make compliance a key part of her brand message, emphasising her commitment to data protection and responsible marketing practices.

She created a clear privacy policy for her website, explaining in plain language how she collected and used data. She also developed a process for regularly auditing her marketing activities to ensure ongoing compliance.

"Remember," the consultant advised, "compliance isn't a one-time thing. It's an ongoing process. You need to stay up-to-date with changes in regulations and regularly review your practices."

Sarah nodded, making a note to schedule quarterly compliance reviews. She realised that while ensuring compliance might seem like extra work, it was actually an opportunity to demonstrate her professionalism and commitment to her clients' best interests.

Pitching to the Pain: The Estate Agent Example

Michelle introduced Sarah to the concept of "pitching to the pain" - addressing the specific challenges of potential referral partners or clients in her marketing.

"Let's take estate agents as an example," Michelle said. "What are the main issues they face when dealing with mortgage brokers?"

Sarah thought for a moment, recalling conversations she'd had with local estate agents. She identified five key pain points:

1. Deals falling through due to financing issues
2. Delays in the buying process caused by slow mortgage approvals
3. Lack of communication from mortgage brokers
4. Inability to help buyers with complex financial situations
5. Lost commissions due to buyers being unable to secure mortgages

Michelle nodded approvingly. "Excellent. Now, how can you address these issues in your pitch to estate agents?"

Sarah worked on crafting a pitch that directly addressed these pain points:

"As a mortgage broker specialising in complex cases, I understand the frustrations you face with financing issues. My service is designed to:

1. Reduce fall-throughs by pre-qualifying buyers thoroughly before they make offers.
2. Speed up the mortgage process with my direct relationships with lenders and efficient application handling.
3. Provide weekly, proactive updates to all parties involved in the transaction.
4. Find solutions for buyers with non-standard income or credit issues, expanding your pool of viable buyers.
5. Increase your successful completions by finding the right mortgage products for a wider range of buyers.

By partnering with me, you can focus on what you do best - selling properties - while I handle all aspects of the mortgage process, ensuring smoother transactions and happier clients."

Sarah realised this approach could be applied to other referral partners too. For solicitors, she could focus on how her efficient mortgage processing could help them meet their conveyancing deadlines. For financial advisors, she could emphasise her expertise in complex cases that complemented their overall financial planning services.

To make her pitch more concrete, Sarah decided to create a one-page "Partnership Benefits" sheet for each type of referral partner. For estate agents, it would include:

- A flowchart showing how her involvement could streamline the buying process
- Statistics on her success rate with complex cases
- Testimonials from other estate agents she had worked with
- A clear outline of her communication process, showing how she'd keep them informed at every stage

She also thought about creating a co-branded "Homebuyer's Guide" that estate agents could give to their clients, positioning herself as a valuable resource, and the estate agent as a well-connected professional.

"This is powerful, Sarah," Michelle said. "By directly addressing their pain points, you're showing these partners that you understand their business and can provide real value. Now, let's think about how you can demonstrate this value in a way that sets you apart from other brokers."

> *Growth Strategy: Revenue problems are rarely actually revenue problems. They're usually symptoms of unclear positioning, weak systems, or team misalignment. Fix the foundation before throwing money at marketing.*

Value Building

Michelle then introduced Sarah to the concept of value building. "By offering a combination of services or benefits that your competitors don't, you make it harder for potential clients to make direct comparisons based solely on rates or fees," Michelle explained.

Sarah brainstormed ways she could build value in her offering:

1. **Mortgage Review Service**: "I could offer an annual review of clients' mortgages to ensure they're always on the best deal," Sarah suggested. She envisioned sending personalised reports to each client on their mortgage anniversary, comparing their current deal to what was available in the market.
2. **Financial Education**: "What about exclusive webinars and workshops on property investment and financial planning for my clients?" Sarah asked. She thought about hosting monthly online sessions, bringing in guest experts to cover topics like tax planning for landlords or strategies for building a property portfolio.
3. **Fast-Track Application**: "I could create a streamlined process for returning clients, reducing paperwork and speeding up approvals," Sarah mused. This could involve keeping detailed records of client information and having a simplified re-application process for those whose circumstances hadn't significantly changed.
4. **Property Market Reports**: "Quarterly reports on local property market trends, exclusive to my clients, could be valuable," Sarah realised. She could compile data on house prices, rental yields, and up-and-coming areas in Manchester, providing insights that would be particularly useful for investors.
5. **Concierge Service**: "I could offer assistance in finding other professionals needed in the home-buying process, like solicitors and surveyors," Sarah thought. She could build a network of trusted professionals, negotiating preferential rates for her clients.

6. **Out-of-Hours Support**: "Availability for consultations outside of normal business hours could set me apart," Sarah considered. She could offer evening and weekend appointments for busy professionals who struggled to meet during standard work hours.

By combining these additional services with her core mortgage broking offering, Sarah created a unique value proposition that set her apart from competitors. She decided to create a "Client Benefits Package" brochure, outlining all these additional services. This would not only attract new clients but also help retain existing ones by demonstrating the ongoing value she provided.

"Remember, Sarah," Michelle advised, "the key is to offer services that are genuinely valuable to your clients and aligned with your expertise. Don't try to be all things to all people - focus on what you can do exceptionally well."

Sarah nodded, feeling excited about the possibilities. She could see how this value-stacked offering would make her services more attractive and harder for competitors to replicate.

Implementing Multi-Channel Marketing Strategies

With her UVP defined, compliance considerations in mind, and value-stacked offering created, Sarah was ready to implement her marketing strategies. She decided to focus on a mix of digital and traditional marketing channels:

1. **Website Optimisation**: Sarah revamped her website to reflect her new brand message. She created separate landing pages for different client segments (first-time buyers, remortgages, buy-to-let investors, etc.), each addressing the specific concerns and needs of that group. For the first-time buyer page, Sarah included:
    - A step-by-step guide to the home-buying process
    - A mortgage affordability calculator

- Testimonials from other first-time buyers she had helped
- A downloadable "First-Time Buyer's Checklist"
- A clear call-to-action for a free initial consultation

She also added a blog section where she could share educational content, and made sure the site was mobile-responsive and fast-loading.

2. **Content Marketing**: Sarah created a content calendar, planning out blog posts, videos, and social media content that would provide value to her potential clients. Example topics included:

   - "5 Things First-Time Buyers in Manchester Need to Know About Mortgages"
   - "How to Improve Your Credit Score for Better Mortgage Rates"
   - "Understanding Buy-to-Let Mortgages: A Guide for New Investors in the Manchester Market"
   - "Remortgaging to Fund Home Improvements: Pros and Cons for Homeowners"

   She committed to creating one in-depth blog post, one video, and several social media posts each week. To make this manageable, she blocked out specific times in her calendar for content creation and batched her efforts, creating several pieces of content in one sitting.

3. **Email Marketing**: Sarah set up an email newsletter, being careful to comply with GDPR requirements for consent. She planned to send monthly updates with market insights, helpful tips, and links to her latest blog posts. Her monthly "Mortgage Market Update" email included:

   - Latest Bank of England base rate news and its impact on mortgages
   - Featured mortgage deals of the month
   - A spotlight on a recent client success story

- Links to her latest educational content
- A clear call-to-action for recipients to book a mortgage review

She used an email marketing platform that allowed her to segment her list, sending tailored content to different groups (e.g., first-time buyers, buy-to-let investors, those nearing remortgage dates).

4. **Social Media**: Sarah chose to focus on LinkedIn and Facebook, where she felt her target audience was most active. She shared a mix of her own content, industry news, and behind-the-scenes glimpses into her work as a broker. On LinkedIn, she posted:

    - Insights on the mortgage market and property industry
    - Success stories (with client permission)
    - Updates on her professional development and industry events she attended

    A sample LinkedIn post: "Just helped a client with a complex income structure secure a mortgage after they were turned down by three high street banks. If you're self-employed or have multiple income sources, don't assume you can't get a mortgage. Let's chat about your options."

    On Facebook, she created a business page and shared:

    - More personal, relatable content about the home-buying journey
    - Tips for first-time buyers and homeowners
    - Local Manchester property news and events

    She also experimented with Facebook Live sessions, hosting monthly Q&As where followers could ask her mortgage-related questions in real-time.

5. **Networking and Partnerships**: Sarah reached out to local estate agents, solicitors, and financial advisors to build referral partnerships. She offered to provide educational content for

their clients in exchange for referrals. She created a "First-Time Buyer's Guide to Mortgages" co-branded with a local estate agent, which the agent could give to all new registered buyers. This guide positioned Sarah as an expert and gave the estate agent valuable content to share with their clients. Sarah also organised a quarterly "Property Professional Networking Event", bringing together various professionals in the property industry. This helped her build relationships and position herself as a connector in the local property scene.

6. **Community Involvement**: Sarah volunteered to give talks at local first-time buyer events and retirement planning seminars. This allowed her to showcase her expertise and connect with potential clients in person. She hosted a monthly "Mortgage Clinic" at a local community centre, offering free 15-minute consultations to anyone with mortgage questions. This not only generated leads but also built goodwill in the community.
7. **Testimonials and Case Studies**: With client permission (and in compliance with GDPR), Sarah began collecting detailed testimonials and creating case studies that demonstrated how she had helped clients in various situations. She created a "Client Success Stories" section on her website, featuring anonymised case studies such as:
   - "How I Helped a Contract Worker Secure a Mortgage for Their Dream Home"
   - "Navigating a Complex Remortgage: A Business Owner's Journey"
   - "From Rejection to Approval: Securing a Mortgage with a Less-Than-Perfect Credit Score"

   Each case study outlined:

   - The client's situation and challenges
   - How Sarah approached the case
   - The solution she found
   - The positive outcome for the client

These stories not only showcased Sarah's expertise but also helped potential clients with similar situations see how she could help them.

By implementing these strategies across multiple channels, Sarah was able to reach a wider audience and reinforce her message of expertise and personalised service. She made sure to maintain a consistent brand voice and message across all platforms, building a strong and recognisable brand in her local market.

As Sarah looked over the comprehensive marketing plan she and Michelle had developed, a wave of apprehension washed over her. The strategies were solid, but the sheer volume of content creation and management seemed overwhelming.

"Michelle," Sarah said, her voice tinged with concern, "this all looks great, but I'm worried about the time commitment. How am I supposed to create all this content, manage social media, and still have time to actually work with clients?"

Michelle nodded understandingly. "That's a valid concern, Sarah. But remember, we're building systems here, not just adding tasks to your plate. One tool that can help significantly is AI."

Sarah raised an eyebrow. "AI? For marketing?"

"Absolutely," Michelle replied. "AI tools can help with content creation, social media management, and even personalised email campaigns. They can generate initial drafts, suggest content ideas, and help optimize your posting schedule."

Sarah leaned forward, intrigued but cautious. "That sounds almost too good to be true. What's the catch?"

Michelle's expression turned serious. "The catch is that while AI can be incredibly helpful, it's not a replacement for the human touch. You need to be very careful to personalise and review anything produced by AI. Your brand voice, your expertise, and your personal touch are what set you apart. AI is a tool to enhance your efforts, not replace them."

Sarah nodded slowly, taking this in. "So, how would this work in practice?"

"Let's take your blog posts as an example," Michelle explained. "You could use AI to generate outlines or first drafts based on topics you choose. But then you'd need to go through and add your personal insights, client anecdotes (anonymised, of course), and ensure the tone aligns with your brand voice. For social media, AI can suggest post ideas and even create draft posts, but you should always review and adjust them to ensure they truly represent you and your brand."

Sarah began to see the potential. "And for email campaigns?"

"AI can help segment your email list and even draft personalised emails for different client groups," Michelle said. "But again, you'll want to review and adjust these to ensure they have that personal touch your clients expect from you."

Michelle continued, "The key is to use AI as a starting point, not an end point. It can help you overcome blank page syndrome and manage the volume of content needed for effective marketing. But your expertise, your voice, and your personal touch are what will truly engage your audience."

Sarah felt a sense of relief mixed with excitement. This approach could help her manage the workload while still maintaining the personal connection she valued with her clients.

"Alright," Sarah said, a new determination in her voice. "Let's look at how we can incorporate AI into our marketing plan, but we'll make sure to build in time for personalisation and review."

Michelle smiled approvingly. "That's the perfect approach, Sarah. We'll use technology to enhance your marketing efforts, not replace your unique value. Now, let's revise this plan to include AI tools, but with clear steps for adding your personal touch to everything we produce."

As they dived back into the marketing plan, Sarah felt a renewed sense of confidence. With AI to help manage the volume and her personal touch to ensure quality and connection, she could see a clear path to implementing a robust, effective marketing strategy without becoming overwhelmed.

"Remember Sarah" Michelle said, "if you can focus on your marketing and really get all these channels working together, you won't just be ahead of your competition, your competition will almost become irrelevant as you'

ll have created a unique offering that your customers can't get elsewhere".

Measuring Marketing Effectiveness

Sarah knew that to continually improve her marketing efforts, she needed to measure their effectiveness. With Michelle's guidance, she set up systems to track key performance indicators (KPIs):

1. Website traffic and engagement (using Google Analytics)
2. Email open rates and click-through rates
3. Social media engagement (likes, shares, comments)
4. Leads generated from each marketing channel
5. Conversion rates from leads to clients
6. Client acquisition cost

She set up a monthly review process to analyse these metrics and adjust her strategies accordingly.

Sarah created a monthly marketing report template:

- Website Traffic: [Number] unique visitors (% change from last month)
- Top Performing Content: [Title] ([Number] page views)
- Email Newsletter: [%] open rate, [%] click-through rate
- Social Media: Top post - [Description] (Reach: [Number])

- Leads Generated: [Number] (Breakdown by channel)
- Conversion Rate: [%] of leads converted to clients
- Client Acquisition Cost: £[Amount] per client

For her first month's report, Sarah filled in the data:

- Website Traffic: 5,000 unique visitors (up 20% from last month)
- Top Performing Content: "Guide to Mortgage Deposits" (1,500 page views)
- Email Newsletter: 35% open rate, 12% click-through rate
- Social Media: LinkedIn post about self-employed mortgages reached 10,000 people
- Leads Generated: 50 (20 from website, 15 from social media, 10 from referrals, 5 from community events)
- Conversion Rate: 30% of leads converted to clients
- Client Acquisition Cost: £200 per client

By regularly reviewing these metrics, Sarah could identify which strategies were most effective and allocate her resources accordingly. She noticed, for example, that her content about self-employed mortgages was performing particularly well, so she decided to create more content targeting this niche.

She also realised that while her community events weren't generating as many leads, the conversion rate from these leads was higher. This led her to consider increasing her community involvement, recognising the value of face-to-face interactions in building trust.

The Ongoing Journey

As the months went by, Sarah found that her marketing efforts were paying off. She was attracting more of her ideal clients - those with complex needs who appreciated her patient, educational approach. Her brand was becoming known in her local area, and she was even starting to get inquiries from outside her usual geographic range due to her online presence.

More importantly, Sarah found that her new marketing approach had transformed her relationship with her clients. By providing value through her content and clearly articulating her unique strengths, she was able to build trust before clients even met her. This led to more productive initial consultations and a higher conversion rate from inquiry to client.

One day, Sarah received an email from a potential client that made her realise just how far she'd come:

"Dear Sarah,

I've been following your blog and social media for a few months now, and I feel like I've learned so much about mortgages already. Your content about self-employed mortgages has been particularly helpful. I'm a freelance graphic designer looking to buy my first home, and I've been worried about getting approved for a mortgage. After reading your case study about how you helped that IT contractor, I feel much more confident. I'd love to schedule a consultation with you to discuss my options.

Thank you for all the valuable information you share, Emma"

Sarah felt a surge of pride as she read the email. This was exactly the kind of client she had hoped to attract with her marketing efforts - someone who had already engaged with her content, understood her value proposition, and was coming to her as a trusted expert rather than just another mortgage broker.

As Sarah's marketing strategies continued to evolve, she noticed several positive changes in her business:

1. **Quality of Leads**: The leads coming in were increasingly aligned with her target market. Potential clients were more informed about the mortgage process and Sarah's unique offerings, leading to more productive initial consultations.
2. **Efficiency**: Because clients had often consumed her educational content before meeting her, Sarah found she

could move through the initial stages of the mortgage process more quickly. Clients came prepared with necessary documents and a better understanding of what to expect.

3. **Referrals**: Sarah's content was being shared not just by clients, but also by other professionals in her network. Estate agents were directing their clients to Sarah's first-time buyer guides, and financial advisors were recommending her to clients with complex income situations.
4. **Brand Recognition**: Sarah was increasingly being recognised as a go-to expert for complex mortgage cases in the Manchester area. She had been invited to speak at several local property investment events and had even been quoted in a regional business publication about mortgage trends.
5. **Work Satisfaction**: By attracting clients who valued her expertise and approach, Sarah found her work more fulfilling. She was able to take on challenging cases that utilised her problem-solving skills and creativity.

However, Sarah also faced some challenges as her marketing efforts expanded:

1. **Time Management**: Creating regular content, managing social media, and responding to increased inquiries was taking up a significant amount of time. Sarah realised she needed to find a balance between marketing activities and client work.
2. **Scaling**: As her reputation grew, Sarah found herself with more leads than she could handle on her own. She began to consider whether it was time to bring on additional staff or perhaps be more selective about the clients she took on.
3. **Staying Current**: The mortgage market was constantly evolving, with new products and regulatory changes. Sarah needed to ensure her content remained up-to-date and accurate.
4. **Measuring ROI**: While Sarah could see the positive impact of her marketing efforts, she found it challenging to accurately measure the return on investment for some of her activities, particularly her community involvement and networking efforts.

To address these challenges, Sarah scheduled another session with Michelle. Together, they developed some strategies:

1. **Content Creation Efficiency**: Sarah decided to batch her content creation, setting aside one day a month to create multiple blog posts and record several videos. She also considered hiring a part-time virtual assistant to help with social media scheduling and email newsletter creation.
2. **Automation**: Sarah invested in marketing automation tools to streamline some of her processes, such as lead nurturing email sequences and social media posting.
3. **Continuous Learning**: Sarah committed to attending at least one industry conference or workshop each quarter to stay updated on market trends and expand her network.
4. **Advanced Analytics**: Michelle introduced Sarah to more sophisticated analytics tools that could help her track the customer journey from initial content interaction through to becoming a client, giving her a clearer picture of which marketing efforts were most effective.

As Sarah implemented these strategies, she found a new rhythm in her business. Her marketing efforts were no longer a separate task she struggled to find time for, but an integral part of her business operations that supported and enhanced her core mortgage broking services.

One year after her marketing overhaul, Sarah sat down to review her progress. The numbers were impressive:

- Website traffic had increased by 300%
- Her email list had grown from 200 to 2,000 subscribers
- She was generating an average of 100 leads per month, up from 20
- Her conversion rate had improved from 25% to 40%
- Her revenue had doubled, while her client acquisition cost had decreased by 30%

But beyond the numbers, Sarah felt a profound sense of achievement. She had built a brand that truly reflected her values and expertise. She was attracting clients she enjoyed working with and making a real difference in their lives. Her business was not just more profitable, but also more fulfilling.

As she looked to the future, Sarah felt excited about the possibilities. She was considering expanding her team to handle the increased demand, perhaps bringing on a junior broker she could mentor. She also had ideas for new content series, including a podcast interviewing local property experts.

Sarah realised that marketing was not just about attracting clients; it was about continuously refining and communicating her value proposition. It was a journey of constant learning and adaptation, much like the mortgage industry itself.

She thought back to the overwhelmed broker she had been just a year ago, struggling to differentiate herself in a crowded market. Now, she had a clear vision of her place in that market and the confidence to continue growing and evolving.

As Sarah closed her laptop and prepared to head home, she felt a sense of excitement for what the next day would bring. She knew there would be challenges ahead, but she also knew she had the tools and mindset to meet them head-on.

The journey of transforming her approach to marketing had not just changed her business; it had changed her as a professional. She was no longer just a mortgage broker; she was a trusted advisor, an educator, and a leader in her field. And she couldn't wait to see where this journey would take her next.

CHAPTER 3 SUMMARY: MARKETING - ATTRACTING YOUR IDEAL CLIENTS

In this chapter, we followed Sarah's journey as she transformed her approach to marketing her company. Key insights and strategies explored include:

1. **Developing a Unique Value Proposition (UVP)**: Sarah discovered the importance of articulating what makes her service unique, focusing on her strengths in patient guidance and creative problem-solving for complex cases.
2. **Client-Centric Marketing**: The chapter emphasized a shift from generic, product-focused marketing to a strategy that highlights the broker's unique strengths and provides real value to potential clients.
3. **Content Marketing**: Sarah developed a content calendar focused on educational articles and videos, positioning herself as a knowledgeable guide in the mortgage process.
4. **Strategic Partnerships**: The importance of building referral partnerships with local Estate Agents and Financial Advisors was highlighted as a key strategy for reaching potential clients.
5. **Multi-Channel Marketing**: Sarah implemented a diverse marketing strategy, including website redesign, content creation, and partnership outreach.
6. **Measuring Marketing Effectiveness**:The chapter stressed the importance of tracking key performance indicators (KPIs) to assess and refine marketing efforts continually.
7. **Consistency in Marketing**: Michelle emphasised the need for ongoing, consistent efforts in marketing to build brand recognition and trust.

8. **Compliance and Regulations**: While not explicitly detailed in the narrative, it's crucial for UK mortgage brokers to ensure all marketing efforts comply with GDPR guidelines and fall within the FCA remit.

The chapter illustrated how effective marketing isn't about promoting a service, but about sharing a passion for helping clients achieve their homeownership dreams, thereby differentiating oneself in a crowded market. Your potential clients need to be reassured that you understand their pain points & have a pain free solution to their issues. Backing this up with testimonials from people in a similar position is key to moving someone form an" interested lead" to a "confirmed customer".

Scan here for the WorkBook

WORKSHEET: ELEVATING YOUR COMPANY MARKETING

Part 1: Crafting Your Unique Value Proposition (UVP)

1. **List three unique strengths of your brokerage:**

   a. ______________________________

   b. ______________________________

   c. ______________________________

2. **Identify three specific needs of your target clients:**

   a. ______________________________

   b. ______________________________

   c. ______________________________

3. **Using the above, craft a compelling UVP for your brokerage (2-3 sentences):**

____

____

____

____

Part 2: Content Marketing Strategy

1. Brainstorm 10 topics for blog posts or videos that would provide value to potential mortgage clients:

    1. ______________________________
    2. ______________________________
    3. ______________________________
    4. ______________________________
    5. ______________________________
    6. ______________________________
    7. ______________________________
    8. ______________________________
    9. ______________________________
    10. ______________________________

2. Choose your top 3 topics and outline a brief content plan for each:

    Topic 1: ______________________________

    Key points to cover:

    - ______________________________
    - ______________________________
    - ______________________________

    Topic 2: ______________________________

    Key points to cover:

    - ______________________________
    - ______________________________
    - ______________________________

Topic 3: ______________________________

Key points to cover:

- ______________________________
- ______________________________
- ______________________________

Part 3: Strategic Partnerships

1. Identify 3 potential strategic partners in your local area:

   a. ______________________________

   b. ______________________________

   c. ______________________________

2. For one of these potential partners, draft a brief outreach message (remember to keep it GDPR compliant). A key learning hear is "pitching to their pain". Identify the three main pains they experience when dealing with someone from your industry then make the pitch based on how you address these pains:

____

____

____

____

Part 4: Marketing Metrics

1. Choose 3-5 key performance indicators (KPIs) to track your marketing efforts:

    a. ______________________________

    b. ______________________________

    c. ______________________________

    d. ______________________________

    e. ______________________________

2. For each KPI, note how you will track it and how often:

____

____

____

____

Part 5: Compliance Check

1. List 3 key GDPR considerations for your marketing efforts:

    a. ______________________________

    b. ______________________________

    c. ______________________________

2. Note 2 FCA guidelines relevant to your marketing strategy:

    a. ______________________________

    b. ______________________________

Part 6: Action Plan

Based on this worksheet, identify 3 concrete actions you will take in the next week to improve your marketing:

1. ______________________________
2. ______________________________
3. ______________________________

Remember, effective marketing is an ongoing process. Regularly revisit and refine your strategy, always ensuring compliance with UK regulations. Your goal is to consistently communicate your unique value to potential clients, positioning yourself as a trusted guide in their mortgage journey.

Part 7: Marketing Calendar

Create a 12 month marketing diary. Firstly start by entering all the public holidays, key events like budgets etc then work from there, filling in video recording days, proposed podcast events etc.

The key to marketing is to work at least three months in advance so that you have time to react to industry or global events as they happen.

For Example: If you are running a Christmas promotion then this needs to be planned in September. By the end of the month you will have ordered stationary & promotional materials, scheduled dates for campaign start and key points etc.

CHAPTER 4:
SALES - CONVERTING LEADS INTO LOYAL CUSTOMERS

"The sole purpose of a business is to win & retain customers. If you create & retain a sufficient number of customers in a cost effective way, the outcome is profit"

Sales Psychology: The best time to ask for a sale is right after you've provided value, not when you need the money. People buy on emotion and justify with logic. Give them both - a story that excites and data that validates.

Sarah took a deep breath, her hand hovering over her phone. She was about to call back a lead who had inquired about remortgaging options, and for the first time, she felt genuinely prepared. Gone were the days of winging it and hoping for the best.

She glanced at the new script she and Michelle had developed, a roadmap for consultative selling tailored specifically for mortgage brokering. It wasn't a rigid set of lines to recite, but a framework to guide her through uncovering the client's true needs and concerns.

As she dialled the number, Sarah reflected on how different this felt from her old approach. Before, she would have launched into a spiel about interest rates and terms, essentially trying to sell a product. Now, she was prepared to have a conversation – to understand the client's situation, goals, and worries before even mentioning a specific mortgage solution.

The phone rang twice before a woman's voice answered. "Hello?"

"Good afternoon, is this Mrs. Johnson?" Sarah asked, her voice warm and professional.

"Yes, it is," came the reply.

"Hi Mrs. Johnson, this is Sarah from Harmony Mortgage Brokers. You reached out to us recently about exploring remortgaging options. I was wondering if this is a good time for us to chat about your property goals?"

There was a pause, then Mrs. Johnson spoke, her tone cautious but interested. "Yes, I suppose now is as good a time as any."

Sarah smiled, settling into her chair. "Wonderful. Before we dive into specific mortgage products, I'd love to understand a bit more about your current situation and what's prompted you to consider remortgaging. Can you tell me a bit about yourself and what you're hoping to achieve?"

As Mrs. Johnson began to speak, Sarah listened intently, jotting down key points. This wasn't just a sales call anymore. It was the beginning of a relationship, one where Sarah could position herself as a trusted advisor rather than just another mortgage broker pushing products.

Sarah: "So, Mrs. Johnson, if I understand correctly, you're considering remortgaging primarily to fund some home improvements, is that right?"

Mrs. Johnson: "Yes, that's the main reason. Our kitchen is desperately in need of an update."

Sarah: "I see. And may I ask, have you considered how long you plan to stay in the property? This can impact the type of remortgage option that might be best for you."

Mrs. Johnson: "Oh, we hadn't really thought about that. I suppose... well, at least another 10 years, I'd say. Our kids are still in school locally."

Sarah: "Thank you, that's really helpful information. Now, regarding the home improvements, do you have a specific budget in mind?"

Mrs. Johnson: "We were thinking around £30,000. Is that reasonable?"

Sarah: "Every situation is unique, but that's certainly a workable figure for many kitchen renovations. Now, let's talk about your current mortgage. Can you tell me a bit about your existing rate and term?"

As the conversation continued, Sarah guided Mrs. Johnson through a series of questions, each one helping to build a clearer picture of her needs and circumstances. By the end of the call, Sarah had all the information she needed to start researching the most suitable remortgage options, and Mrs. Johnson felt heard and understood.

The Consultative Selling Approach

After the call, Sarah leaned back in her chair, feeling a sense of accomplishment. She realized that this new approach to sales wasn't just about closing deals – it was about building trust and providing real value to her clients.

Sarah reflected on the key elements of the consultative selling approach that Michelle had taught her:

1. **Active Listening**: Instead of thinking about what to say next, Sarah had focused on truly hearing Mrs. Johnson's needs and concerns.

2. **Asking Probing Questions**: Each question Sarah asked was designed to uncover deeper insights about Mrs. Johnson's situation and goals.
3. **Educating the Client**: Throughout the conversation, Sarah had taken opportunities to provide valuable information, helping Mrs. Johnson understand the remortgaging process better.
4. **Tailoring Solutions**: By gathering comprehensive information, Sarah knew she could now research and present options that truly fit Mrs. Johnson's unique situation.
5. **Building Trust**: By focusing on understanding rather than selling, Sarah had begun to establish herself as a trusted advisor in Mrs. Johnson's eyes.

Sarah opened her notebook and began to jot down her thoughts on how this approach differed from her old sales techniques:

Old Approach	**New Consultative Approach**
Focus on product features	Focus on client needs and goals
Talking at the client	Conversing with the client
One-size-fits-all pitch	Tailored approach for each client
Emphasis on closing the sale	Emphasis on building a relationship
Reactive to client questions	Proactively educating the client

As she looked at this comparison, Sarah felt a renewed sense of purpose. She wasn't just selling mortgages; she was helping people make one of the most significant financial decisions of their lives.

Developing a Repeatable Sales Process

The next day, Sarah met with Michelle to discuss how to turn this new approach into a repeatable process.

Michelle: "Sarah, I'm glad to hear your call with Mrs. Thompson went so well. Now, let's talk about how we can systematise this approach so you can consistently deliver this level of service to all your clients."

Sarah nodded eagerly. "I'd love that. I feel like I've just been winging it for so long, even with this new approach."

Michelle smiled. "That's normal. Many brokers rely solely on their intuition. But having a structured process doesn't mean losing your personal touch – it means ensuring you consistently cover all bases and provide value to every client."

Together, they mapped out a sales process for Sarah's brokerage:

1. **Initial Contact**: Respond to inquiries promptly, schedule a consultation.
2. **Preparation**: Review any available information about the client before the call or meeting.
3. **Discovery Call/Meeting**: Use the consultative selling approach to understand the client's needs, goals, and circumstances.At this stage introduce the needs for protection products as part of the client's considerations.
4. **Needs Analysis**: After the call, analyse the information gathered and identify potential solutions.
5. **Research and Solution Development**: Research suitable mortgage options based on the client's needs.
6. **Presentation of Options**: Present tailored options to the client, explaining pros and cons of each.
7. **Address Concerns and Objections**: Use knowledge and empathy to address any client concerns.
8. **Agreement and Application**: Once the client is comfortable, proceed with the chosen option and begin the application process.
9. **Follow-up and Support**: Provide regular updates throughout the application process and be available for any questions.
10. **Post-Completion Care**: Check in with the client after completion to ensure satisfaction and maintain the relationship.

Sarah looked at this process, feeling a mix of excitement and apprehension. "This looks great, Michelle, but it also seems like a lot to remember for every client."

Michelle nodded understandingly. "That's where tools and systems come in. Let's talk about how we can support this process with the right tools."

Implementing Sales Tools and Systems

Over the next few weeks, Sarah worked on implementing tools and systems to support her new sales process:

1. **Customer Relationship Management (CRM) System**: Sarah chose a CRM tailored for mortgage brokers. She set it up to track each client's journey through her sales process, set reminders for follow-ups, and store important client information.
2. **Needs Analysis Questionnaire**: Sarah developed a comprehensive questionnaire to ensure she gathered all necessary information during discovery calls. She loaded this into her CRM to easily record responses during calls.
3. **Product Comparison Tool**: Sarah invested in a mortgage product comparison tool that allowed her to quickly identify suitable options based on client needs.
4. **Email Templates**: She created a series of email templates for different stages of the sales process, from initial follow-up to application updates. These ensured consistent communication while saving time.
5. **Objection Handling Guide**: Sarah compiled a document of common client objections and effective ways to address them, keeping it handy for quick reference during calls. She also created a client video that addressed the most common objections along with a clear explanation on how Harmony Mortgages addressed these concerns.
6. **Client Education Materials**: She developed a series of simple, clear documents explaining various mortgage concepts and processes. These could be sent to clients as needed to support their decision-making.

As Sarah integrated these tools into her daily work, she found that her efficiency improved dramatically. She was able to handle more clients without sacrificing the personal touch that was so important to her approach.

Growing Pains and Emotional Turmoil

As Sarah implemented her new sales approach, she found herself riding an emotional rollercoaster. Some days, she felt on top of the world, confidently guiding clients through complex mortgage decisions. Other days, she questioned whether she was cut out for this level of business growth.

One particularly challenging week, Sarah found herself overwhelmed with the influx of new leads generated by her improved marketing efforts. She had been up until 2 AM for three nights straight, trying to keep up with follow-ups and proposal preparations. As she stared at her computer screen, bleary-eyed and exhausted, a wave of doubt washed over her.

Sarah picked up her phone and dialled Michelle's number, not caring that it was barely 7 AM.

"Sarah? Is everything alright?" Michelle's voice was alert despite the early hour.

"I don't know if I can do this, Michelle," Sarah blurted out, her voice cracking. "I'm drowning in leads, I haven't seen my family properly in days, and I'm terrified I'm going to let clients down because I can't keep up."

Michelle's tone softened. "Take a deep breath, Sarah. What you're feeling is normal. Growing a business isn't just about systems and strategies – it's an emotional journey too."

Sarah felt tears welling up. "But I thought I had it all figured out. The new systems, the consultative approach – it's all working, but I feel like I'm falling apart."

"Success often brings its own challenges," Michelle said gently. "Let's meet for coffee in an hour. We'll work through this together."

An hour later, Sarah sat across from Michelle in a quiet café, clutching a steaming mug of coffee like a lifeline.

Michelle leaned forward; her eyes filled with understanding but also a steely determination. "Sarah, you've come so far, and you're doing amazing work. But it's clear we need to address the next challenge – scaling your success sustainably."

Sarah nodded, feeling a mix of relief at being heard and apprehension about what came next.

"Here's the hard truth," Michelle continued, her tone firm but kind. "You can't continue to do everything yourself. Your business is growing, and that's fantastic. But if you don't learn to delegate and build a team, you'll burn out. And that won't serve you or your clients."

Sarah felt a knot in her stomach. "But how can I trust anyone else to handle these important client relationships? What if they make mistakes?"

Michelle smiled. "That's a common fear. But remember, you've built solid systems and processes. With the right training, you can empower others to deliver the same level of service you pride yourself on."

Sarah nodded slowly, considering Michelle's suggestion. But then a worried frown creased her brow. "An assistant and a junior broker? Michelle, I'm not sure I can afford that, especially the assistant. That seems like a big expense when I'm already feeling stretched."

Michelle leaned back in her chair, a thoughtful expression on her face. "Let's break this down, Sarah. What's your average case size in terms of commission?"

Sarah thought for a moment. "About £1,620."

"Okay, good," Michelle nodded. "Now, think back to your weekly time study. How much time did you spend doing work that only a qualified mortgage adviser could achieve?"

Sarah reflected on her packed schedule. "Well, when I really think about it, probably only about six hours per case. That includes the discovery call, the fact-find - which I'm now automating - sourcing products, and making the recommendation."

Michelle's eyes lit up. "Excellent. So that equates to £270 per hour when you're doing mortgage adviser work. Now, how much time in your week did you spend on administrative work?"

Sarah winced. "About 44 hours, I'd say."

"And how much would a decent administrator cost, do you think?"

They discussed it and settled on a figure of £28,000 per annum, which worked out to about £18 per hour for a full-time administrator.

Michelle leaned forward, her gaze intent. "So, Sarah, let me put this to you: You're sacrificing time with your family and time doing mortgage adviser work at £270 per hour so you can save £18 per hour by not paying a good quality administrator. You need to value your time."

Sarah sat back, stunned. When Michelle put it like that, it seemed so clear. She had been so focused on the outgoing cost that she hadn't considered the opportunity cost of her time.

"I... I never thought of it that way," Sarah admitted.

Michelle smiled gently. "Many business owners fall into this trap. They try to do everything themselves to save money but end up limiting their earning potential and burning themselves out in the process."

Sarah nodded, a new understanding dawning. "So, by hiring an administrator, I could potentially take on more clients, or at least focus on the parts of the business that really require my expertise."

"Exactly," Michelle confirmed. "And don't forget the intangible benefits - less stress, more time with your family, and the ability to focus on growing your business strategically rather than just keeping up with day-to-day tasks."

Sarah felt a weight lift from her shoulders. The idea of delegating still made her a bit nervous, but now she could see the clear benefits - not just for her business, but for her quality of life as well.

"Okay," Sarah said, her voice filled with new determination. "Let's do this. Can you help me create a job description for an administrator?"

Michelle beamed. "Of course. And while we're at it, let's also outline a plan for gradually delegating tasks. Remember, this is a process. You don't have to hand everything over at once."

As they began to sketch out plans for hiring and training an assistant, Sarah felt a renewed sense of excitement about her business's future. She realized that this was the next step in her journey - not just being a great mortgage broker but becoming a true business leader.

Over the next hour, Michelle guided Sarah through a plan to hire and train an assistant and a junior broker. They discussed strategies for gradual delegation, starting with administrative tasks and slowly progressing to client interactions.

As they wrapped up their impromptu session, Sarah felt a weight lift from her shoulders. The path forward still seemed challenging, but no longer impossible.

"Thank you, Michelle," Sarah said, her voice steadier than it had been in days. "I don't know what I'd do without you as a sounding board."

Michelle reached across the table and squeezed Sarah's hand. "That's what I'm here for. Remember, building a business is a marathon, not a sprint. It's okay to have doubts and struggles along the way. What matters is how you respond to them."

In the weeks that followed, Sarah faced numerous challenges as she began to build her team. There were moments of frustration when her new assistant misunderstood a client's needs, and times of pride when her junior broker successfully closed their first deal.

Through it all, Michelle remained a constant source of support and guidance. She celebrated Sarah's victories, no matter how small, and provided a voice of reason during moments of doubt. When Sarah hesitated to delegate an important client meeting to her junior broker, Michelle firmly reminded her of the importance of trust and growth.

"If you don't give them the opportunity to rise to the challenge, how will they – or you – ever grow?" Michelle had asked, her tone leaving no room for argument.

As Sarah's team slowly but surely came together, she found a new rhythm in her work. The long nights became less frequent, and she was able to focus more on strategic growth and complex cases that truly required her expertise.

One evening, as Sarah locked up the office at a reasonable hour for the first time in months, she felt a sense of accomplishment wash over her. She pulled out her phone and sent a quick text to Michelle:

"Just heading home to have dinner with my family. Thank you for believing in me, even when I didn't believe in myself. I couldn't have done this without you."

Michelle's reply came quickly: "You did the hard work, Sarah. I just helped you see what you were capable of. Enjoy your evening – you've earned it."

As Sarah drove home, she reflected on how far she'd come. The journey hadn't been easy, and she knew there would be more challenges ahead. But with her new sales approach, a growing team, and Michelle's unwavering support, she felt ready to face whatever came next.

The transformation of her sales process had done more than improve her business metrics – it had changed her as a person and as a leader. Sarah was no longer just a mortgage broker; she was a business owner, a mentor to her team, and a trusted advisor to her clients. And she was excited to see where this journey would take her next.

Mastering the Art of Follow-Up

One area where Sarah had always struggled was consistent follow-up. She often found herself so busy with active clients that leads, and past clients fell by the wayside. Michelle emphasised the importance of a systematic follow-up process.

Michelle: "Sarah, in all businesses, timing is everything. A lead who isn't ready now might be perfect in six months. And past clients can be a goldmine for repeat business and referrals."

Sarah nodded, thinking of all the potential clients she might have lost due to poor follow-up. "So how do I manage this without spending all my time chasing leads?"

Michelle smiled. "It's all about having a system. Let's create a follow-up schedule that you can implement with your CRM."

Together, they developed a follow-up system:

1. **New Leads:**
    - Welcome to Harmony Mortgages email with video embedded
    - Immediate response within 2 hours
    - If no response, follow up after 1 day, then 3 days, then 1 week
    - If still no response, move to monthly follow-up list

2. **Post-Discovery Call:**
    - Send a summary email within 24 hours. Email contains an embedded video explaining the next steps in a mortgage application process.
    - If no decision made, follow up after 3 days, then 1 week, then 2 weeks.
3. **During Application Process:**
    - Update client at least weekly.
    - Immediate communication for any issues or required information.
    - Email with embedded video for every milestone reached with the purpose of explain what stage has been reached and what will be the next steps.
4. **Post-Completion:**
    - Check-in call 1 week after completion.
    - Follow-up call after 1 month.
    - Add to quarterly newsletter list.
    - Annual check-in call.
5. **Past Clients & clients not ready to proceed:**
    - Quarterly newsletter with market updates and helpful tips.
    - Annual review call to check if circumstances have changed.
    - Birthday and holiday cards to maintain personal connection.

Sarah set up these follow-up schedules in her CRM, with automated reminders to ensure she stayed on track. She also created email templates for each follow-up stage, making it easy to maintain consistent communication.

Handling Objections with Confidence

As Sarah implemented her new sales process, she found that she was better prepared for client objections. However, she still sometimes struggled with particularly challenging situations. Michelle suggested they do some role-playing to practice handling difficult objections.

Michelle: "Okay, Sarah, let's say I'm a potential client. You've just presented some remortgage options to me, and I say, 'These rates are higher than I've seen advertised by several banks. Why should I go through a broker?'"

Sarah took a deep breath, then responded: "That's a great question, and I'm glad you brought it up. While it's true that banks sometimes advertise very low headline rates, these are often only available to a small percentage of borrowers with perfect credit scores and straightforward financial situations. As a broker, I have access to a wide range of lenders, including specialist lenders who might offer better overall deals for your specific circumstances.

"Additionally, the advertised rate isn't the only factor to consider. There are also fees, terms, and flexibility to think about. My role is to look at your entire financial picture and find the best overall solution, not just the lowest headline rate. I can often find deals that you might not have access to directly, and I'll advocate on your behalf with lenders.

"Lastly, I provide personalised support throughout the entire process, from application to completion. This level of service and expertise often leads to a smoother, less stressful experience. Would you like me to walk you through how the total cost of the options I've presented compares to the bank rates you've seen?"

Michelle nodded approvingly. "Excellent response, Sarah. You addressed the concern, educated the client about the value you provide, and offered to provide more detailed information. Let's practice a few more scenarios."

They spent the next hour role-playing various objections, from concerns about fees to doubts about affordability criteria. With each scenario, Sarah grew more confident in her ability to address client concerns effectively.

> *"Pretend that every single person you meet has a sign around his or her neck that says, 'Make me feel important.' Not only will you succeed in sales, you'll succeed in life."*
> *– Mary Kay Ash*

The Power of Social Proof

As Sarah's new sales approach began to yield results, Michelle suggested leveraging these successes to further enhance her sales process.

Michelle: "Sarah, you're doing great work for your clients. Have you considered how you might use their experiences to help convince potential clients?"

Sarah looked puzzled. "You mean like testimonials?"

Michelle nodded. "Exactly. Social proof can be a powerful tool in your sales process. When potential clients hear about positive experiences from people in similar situations, it can help build trust and overcome hesitations."

Together, they brainstormed ways to incorporate social proof into Sarah's sales process:

1. **Case Studies**: Sarah would create detailed case studies of successful client outcomes, anonymising personal details but providing enough information to show how she solved complex problems.
2. **Testimonial Collection**: She would implement a system to collect testimonials from satisfied clients, focusing on the specific ways she had helped them.

3. **Video Testimonials**: For willing clients, Sarah would record short video testimonials to use on her website and in presentations.
4. **Industry Awards and Certifications**: Sarah would prominently display any industry recognition or advanced certifications she received, demonstrating her expertise.
5. **Social Media Showcasing**: She would share (with permission) positive client outcomes and testimonials on her professional social media profiles.

Sarah began to incorporate these elements into her sales presentations and marketing materials. She found that sharing relevant case studies during client meetings helped potential clients understand the value she could provide in concrete terms.

Continual Improvement and Adaptation

As the months passed, Sarah found that her new sales approach was yielding significant results. Her conversion rate had improved, and she was receiving more referrals from satisfied clients. However, she also realised that the sales process wasn't static – it needed continual refinement and adaptation.

Sarah began to hold monthly review sessions, analysing her sales data and client feedback to identify areas for improvement. She paid attention to which types of clients were converting at higher rates, which objections were coming up most frequently, and which parts of her process seemed to resonate most with clients.

She also stayed attuned to changes in the mortgage market, adjusting her approach as new products became available or lending criteria changed. Sarah realised that staying informed and adaptable was key to maintaining her edge in a competitive industry.

One day, as Sarah successfully closed a particularly challenging case, she reflected on how far she'd come. She no longer saw sales as a necessary evil or a process of convincing reluctant clients.

Instead, she viewed it as a collaborative process of understanding needs and finding the best solutions. She was no longer just a mortgage broker – she was a trusted advisor, guiding clients through one of the most significant financial decisions of their lives.

As Sarah picked up the phone to make her next call, she felt a sense of purpose and confidence. She knew that with her consultative approach, robust process, and genuine desire to help, she was well-equipped to serve her clients and grow her business. The transformation of her sales approach had not just improved her business metrics – it had revolutionised her entire perspective on her role as a mortgage broker.

CHAPTER 4 SUMMARY: SALES - CONVERTING LEADS INTO LOYAL CUSTOMERS

In this chapter, we followed Sarah's journey as she transformed her sales approach from a product-centric model to a client-centric, consultative process. Key insights and strategies explored include:

1. **Consultative Selling Approach**: Sarah learned to focus on understanding client needs and goals rather than pushing products, positioning herself as a trusted advisor.
2. **Developing a Repeatable Sales Process**: The chapter outlined a structured 10-step process from initial contact to post-completion care, ensuring consistency and thoroughness in client interactions.
3. **Implementing Sales Tools and Systems**: Sarah integrated various tools including a CRM system, needs analysis questionnaire, and product comparison tools to support her sales process.
4. **Mastering the Art of Follow-Up**: A systematic follow-up process was developed, covering new leads, ongoing applications, and past clients to maintain relationships and capture opportunities.
5. **Handling Objections with Confidence**: Through role-playing and preparation, Sarah improved her ability to address client concerns effectively.
6. **Leveraging Social Proof**: The chapter explored ways to use client testimonials, case studies, and industry recognition to build trust with potential clients.
7. **Continual Improvement and Adaptation**: Sarah learned the importance of regularly reviewing and refining her sales process based on data and feedback.

The chapter illustrated how a well-structured, client-focused sales approach can not only improve business metrics but also transform a mortgage broker's entire perspective on their role, leading to more fulfilling client relationships and business growth.

Scan here for the WorkBook

WORKSHEET: ELEVATING YOUR SALES PROCESS

Part 1: Assessing Your Current Sales Approach

Rate your current approach on a scale of 1-10 (1 being lowest, 10 highest):

1. How client-centric is your sales process? ___
2. How consistent is your approach across different clients? ___
3. How effective are you at uncovering client needs? ___
4. How confident are you in handling objections? ___
5. How systematic is your follow-up process? ___

Part 2: Developing Your Consultative Selling Approach

1. List 5 open-ended questions you can ask to better understand a client's situation and goals:

   a. ______________________________

   b. ______________________________

   c. ______________________________

   d. ______________________________

   e. ______________________________

2. Describe your unique value proposition as a mortgage broker. What sets you apart from others?

____

____

____

____

Part 3: Crafting Your Sales Process

Outline the steps in your ideal sales process, from initial contact to post-completion:

1. ____
2. ____
3. ____
4. ____
5. ____
6. ____
7. ____
8. ____
9. ____
10. ____

Part 4: Handling Objections

List 3 common objections you face and how you would address them:

1. Objection: _______________________________________

   Response: _______________________________________

2. Objection: ____

   Response: ____

3. Objection: ____

   Response: ____

Part 5: Implementing Follow-Up Strategies

Design a follow-up schedule for:

1. New Leads:

____

____

____

____

2. Ongoing Applications:

____

____

____

____

3. Past Clients:

____

____

____

____

Part 6: Leveraging Social Proof

1. List 3 client success stories you could develop into case studies:

    a. ______________________________

    b. ______________________________

    c. ______________________________

2. Draft a request for a client testimonial:

____

____

____

____

Part 7: Sales Tools and Systems

1. What CRM system do you use (or plan to use)?

____

____

____

____

2. List 3 key features you need in a mortgage product comparison tool:

    a. ______________________________

    b. ______________________________

    c. ______________________________

Part 8: Continual Improvement

1. How often will you review your sales process? __________

   ____

2. List 3 key performance indicators (KPIs) you'll track to measure the effectiveness of your sales process:

   a. ____

   b. ____

   c. ____

Part 9: Action Plan

Based on this worksheet, identify 3 immediate actions you will take to improve your sales process:

1. ____
2. ____
3. ____

Remember, transforming your sales process is an ongoing journey. Regularly revisit this worksheet to assess your progress and identify areas for further improvement. Your goal is to consistently provide value to your clients, positioning yourself as a trusted advisor in their mortgage journey.

CHAPTER 5:

OPERATIONS - STREAMLINING YOUR BUSINESS

"Practice the philosophy of continuous improvement. Get a little bit better every single day."
~Brian Tracy

Staff Motivation: When giving feedback, people remember 20% of what went wrong and 80% of how you made them feel. Focus more on the emotional delivery than the technical details. A harsh truth wrapped in empathy goes much further than cold criticism.

Sarah stood in her office, surveying the scene with a mixture of pride and amazement. Gone were the piles of paper that once cluttered every surface. Her desk, once a maze of sticky notes and random files, now held only her computer, a neatly organised planner, and a single file for her current client meeting.

She clicked open her new CRM system, marvelling at how it had transformed her daily operations. Each client's journey was clearly mapped out, from initial inquiry to loan completion.

Automated reminders ensured no follow-up was missed; no deadline overlooked.

As she prepared for her morning team meeting - yes, she had a team now - Sarah reflected on the journey that had brought her here. The process of streamlining her operations had been challenging, often frustrating, but the results were undeniable.

Her new assistant, Emma, popped her head around the door. "Morning, Sarah. The team's ready for the huddle. Oh, and the Johnson file is prepped for your review, and I've scheduled the call with the Garcias for 2 pm, as requested."

Sarah nodded, feeling a wave of calm wash over her. "Thanks, Emma. I'll be right there."

As she walked to the meeting room, Sarah couldn't help but compare this moment to those frantic mornings just a few months ago. She wasn't just working in her business anymore. She was directing it, with clear processes and systems that allowed her and her team to focus on what really mattered - helping clients achieve their property dreams.

The transformation in her operations hadn't just made her more efficient; it had given her the freedom to grow, to innovate, and to rediscover the passion that had led her to become a mortgage broker in the first place.

Sarah: "Alright team, let's start with our daily huddle. Emma, can you give us an update on our pipeline?"

Emma: "Certainly. We have three applications pending approval, two that just entered the underwriting stage, and five new inquiries from yesterday that need initial consultations scheduled."

Sarah: "Great. Tom, how are we looking on those pending approvals?"

Tom: "I've been in touch with the lenders on all three. The Smiths' application should be approved by end of day. The other two might need some additional documentation."

Sarah: "Okay, let's make sure we're proactive on those. What do we need, and who's reaching out to the clients?"

Tom: "I've already sent automated requests through our system. Clients have been notified that they'll need to upload the documents by tomorrow to avoid delays."

Sarah: "Perfect. That's exactly why we implemented this system. Lisa, how are you managing the new inquiries?"

Lisa: "I've sent out our welcome packs and scheduled initial calls for three of them already. The other two I'll be contacting this morning."

Sarah: "Excellent work, everyone. Remember, our goal is to make this process as smooth as possible for our clients. If you encounter any bottlenecks or have ideas for improvement, don't hesitate to bring them up. Now, let's talk about our focus for the day..."

> *"For things to change, YOU have to change.*
> *For things to get better, YOU have to get better.*
> *For things to improve, YOU need to improve.*
> *When YOU grow, everything in your life grows with you".*
> *Jim Rohn*

The Journey to Operational Excellence

As the team dispersed after the huddle, Sarah took a moment to reflect on the journey that had brought her to this point. It hadn't been an easy road, but the transformation in her business was undeniable.

She remembered the day, not too long ago, when she had sat down with her coach, Michelle, feeling overwhelmed and unsure how to move forward.

(Flashback to Sarah's coaching session with Michelle)

Sarah: "Michelle, I feel like I'm drowning in paperwork and admin tasks. I became a mortgage broker to help people, but I spend more time fighting my own systems than actually working with clients."

Michelle nodded understandingly. "Sarah, what you're experiencing is common among business owners who've grown their company's to a certain point. You've been successful, which is great, but now your operations aren't keeping up with your growth. Let's talk about how we can change that."

Sarah leaned forward, eager to hear more.

Michelle continued, "The key is to build repeatable quality into your operations. This can only happen through systemisation. We need to create processes that are consistent, efficient, and scalable."

Sarah looked puzzled. "Systemisation? Doesn't that sound a bit... impersonal? I pride myself on giving personalised service to each client."

Michelle smiled. "That's a common misconception. Systemisation doesn't mean treating every client the same. It means creating a framework that ensures consistency in your service quality, frees up your time for meaningful client interactions, and allows your business to grow without sacrificing that personal touch."

Sarah nodded slowly, beginning to understand. "Okay, so where do we start?"

Michelle pulled out a notebook. "Let's begin by mapping out your current processes. We'll identify bottlenecks, redundancies, and areas where technology could help. Then, we'll work on creating standard operating procedures for each key area of your business."

And so began Sarah's journey towards operational excellence.

Step 1: Process Mapping

Sarah and Michelle spent the next few sessions meticulously mapping out every process in Sarah's brokerage. They started with the client journey, from initial inquiry to loan completion and beyond.

Sarah was shocked to see how many unnecessary steps and redundancies existed in her current processes. Simple tasks like sending follow-up emails or scheduling appointments were eating up hours of her time each week.

Michelle introduced Sarah to flowcharting techniques, helping her create visual representations of each process. This exercise alone was eye-opening for Sarah.

Sarah: "I had no idea I was doing so many things manually that could be automated. No wonder I feel like I'm always playing catch-up!"

Michelle: "Exactly. Now that we can see the entire process laid out, let's start identifying areas for improvement."

They went through each flowchart, marking areas where:

1. Tasks could be automated
2. Steps could be eliminated or combined
3. Technology could be leveraged
4. Team members could be better utilised

By the end of this exercise, Sarah had a clear picture of her operational inefficiencies and a roadmap for improvement.

Step 2: Technology Integration

With a clear understanding of her processes, Sarah was ready to explore how technology could streamline her operations.

Michelle: "Sarah, there are many tools out there designed specifically for mortgage brokers. The key is to choose ones that integrate well with each other and align with your specific needs."

They researched various options, focusing on:

1. Customer Relationship Management (CRM) System: To manage client information, track interactions, and automate follow-ups.
2. Document Management System: To securely store and easily retrieve client documents.
3. Mortgage Comparison Tool: To quickly identify suitable products for clients.
4. Task Management Software: To assign and track tasks within the team.
5. Digital Signature Solution: To facilitate remote document signing.

Sarah was initially overwhelmed by the options, but Michelle guided her through the selection process, emphasising the importance of user-friendliness and scalability.

After careful consideration, Sarah chose a comprehensive CRM system that integrated most of these functions. The implementation process was challenging, requiring her to input all her client data and adapt to new ways of working. But as she became more familiar with the system, she began to see its benefits.

Sarah: "It's amazing. I can see a client's entire history at a glance, set automated reminders for follow-ups, and even track which marketing channels are bringing in the most leads."

Michelle: "That's great, Sarah. Remember, the goal of technology is to support and enhance your operations, not to replace the personal touch that makes your service unique."

> *Customer Psychology: When a client is angry, they don't want a solution first - they want validation. Spend 80% of the time acknowledging their frustration and 20% solving the problem. Rushing to fix before listening often backfires.*

Step 3: Creating Standard Operating Procedures (SOPs)

With her processes mapped and technology in place, Sarah was ready to document her new, improved workflows into Standard Operating Procedures (SOPs).

Michelle explained the importance of SOPs: "These documents will ensure consistency in your service delivery, make training new team members easier, and allow you to step away from the business without everything falling apart."

Sarah and Michelle worked on creating SOPs for key processes, including:

1. New Client Onboarding
2. Loan Application Submission
3. Document Collection and Verification
4. Client Communication Protocols
5. Lender Communication Processes
6. Application Tracking and Follow-up
7. Post-Completion Client Care

For each SOP, they included:

- Step-by-step instructions
- Screenshots of relevant software interfaces
- Explainer videos
- Checklists for quality control
- Tips for handling common issues

Sarah found the process of creating SOPs enlightening. "I'm realising how much of my process was in my head. Writing it down is forcing me to really think through each step and find ways to make it more efficient."

Michelle nodded. "Exactly. And now, anyone on your team can follow these procedures and deliver the same high-quality service you would."

As Harmony Mortgages continued to grow, Sarah found herself increasingly worried about losing the personal touch that had been a cornerstone of her business from the beginning. She had always prided herself on building meaningful relationships with both clients and introducers, remembering small details about their lives and going the extra mile to show her appreciation. However, with the expanding client base and team, she felt like she was losing that connection.

During one of their regular coaching sessions, Sarah expressed her concerns to Michelle.

"I feel like we're becoming too corporate," Sarah admitted, her brow furrowed. "I used to know every client's story, their childrens' names, their dreams. Now, I'm afraid we're just becoming another faceless financial institution."

Michelle nodded understandingly. "It's a common concern as businesses grow, Sarah. But there are ways to maintain that personal touch, even at scale. Have you considered creating a role specifically dedicated to nurturing these relationships?"

Sarah looked intrigued. "What do you mean?"

"I'm thinking of something like a Client Satisfaction Manager," Michelle explained. "This person would be responsible for knowing as much as possible about your clients, introducers, and potential introducers. They would ensure that Harmony maintains that personal connection you've always valued."

Sarah's eyes lit up. "That sounds perfect! But how would it work in practice?"

Michelle leaned forward; her enthusiasm evident. "It's about more than just sending birthday cards, although that's part of it. This person would be responsible for really understanding what matters to each client and introducer. They'd keep track of significant events in their lives, their preferences, their challenges. Then, they'd work with the rest of the team to show that Harmony truly cares."

Sarah nodded slowly, ideas already forming. "So, we could do things like..."

"Exactly," Michelle smiled. "Let me give you a few examples of how this has worked for other businesses I've coached."

Example 1: The Marathon Runner "There was a mortgage broker who found out that one of their key introducers, an estate agent, was training for their first marathon. The Client Satisfaction Manager arranged for the company to sponsor the agent's run, providing custom-made running gear with both the agent's name and the mortgage company's logo. They also set up a cheer station along the marathon route with staff members supporting the agent. The introducer was so touched by this personal level of support that they became one of the company's strongest advocates, significantly increasing their referrals."

Example 2: The New Parents "Another example was a client who had just had their first child shortly after completing their mortgage. The Client Satisfaction Manager noted this and arranged for a beautiful, personalised baby book to be sent to the clients, with a heartfelt note congratulating them on both their new home and their new family member. The clients were so moved by this gesture that they've referred multiple friends and family members to the brokerage since then."

Example 3:The Business Milestone "A third instance involved an introducer, an accountant, who was celebrating their firm's 25th anniversary. The mortgage company's Client Satisfaction Manager worked with a local artist to create a beautiful, custom piece of art featuring the accountant's firm logo and significant milestones. They presented this at the accountant's anniversary party, along with a heartfelt speech about their partnership. This gesture so impressed the accountant and their team that they made the mortgage company their exclusive referral partner for all their clients' mortgage needs."

Sarah sat back, her mind racing with possibilities. "This is exactly what I've been missing! It's not about grand gestures, it's about really knowing our clients and introducers, and showing them, we care in meaningful ways."

Michelle nodded, pleased to see Sarah's enthusiasm. "Exactly. By creating this role, you're making a commitment to maintaining those personal relationships, no matter how large Harmony grows. It becomes a part of your company culture, not just something you do when you have time."

Sarah was already jotting down notes. "We could start by reviewing our current client and introducer base, identifying key events or interests we might have missed. And for new clients, we could make this personal touch a part of our onboarding process."

"That's a great place to start," Michelle agreed. "Remember, the goal is to make each client and introducer feel valued and understood. It's about creating a connection that goes beyond just business transactions."

Then Sarah's face dropped a little and the initial eagerness dissipated.

"Sarah, tell me what you are thinking?" Michelle enquired.

Sarah sheepishly responded "Cost.... this is a lovely idea & I'm fully on board, but this person is going to need paying, then there's the added expense of these gestures. I simply don't know where the budget would come from".

Michelle smiled a knowing smile. "I'm glad you're thinking of the financials Sarah and we do need to monetise the role to cover the increase in costs, but the role is not all about increasing the experience of those we already work with, it also applies to those we would still love to build new relationships with.

If your Client Satisfaction Manager had a list of your top 50 dream strategic partners, and part of their role was learning as much about these people, not only their businesses but also hobbies & interests, they would soon have a valuable database to be working. They could then start reaching out to build relationships with these people and, eventually set meetings for you to meet with them.

If we tasked them with landing you one new quality strategic partner each quarter, & we'll set "quality" as a business that can introduce sufficient leads to result in 10 completed mortgages per month, would your Client Satisfaction Manager be covering their wages?"

The initial excitement returned to Sarah's face, "most definitely they would".

As their session wound down, Sarah felt a renewed sense of purpose. She realised that growth didn't have to mean losing the personal touch that had made Harmony special. With the right systems and people in place, they could continue to build meaningful relationships, no matter how large they became.

"Thank you, Michelle," Sarah said as they wrapped up. "I think this Client Satisfaction Manager role might be the key to maintaining our identity as we grow."

Michelle smiled. "I'm glad it resonates with you. Remember, at the end of the day, people do business with people, not corporations. By maintaining these personal connections, you're not just building a business – you're building a community."

Sarah left the session feeling energized and focused. She couldn't wait to start implementing this new role and finding more ways to show their clients and introducers just how much Harmony valued them. She knew that this commitment to personal relationships would set Harmony apart in an increasingly competitive market.

Step 4: Building a Team and Delegating

As Sarah's systems became more organised, she realised she had the capacity to take on more clients. But to do so without sacrificing quality, she needed to build a team.

Michelle guided Sarah through the process of identifying roles she needed to fill, writing job descriptions, and conducting interviews. However, Sarah quickly realised that recruiting the right people was more challenging than she had anticipated.

Sarah's initial approach to interviews was haphazard at best. She would often do most of the talking, enthusiastically selling the benefits of working for her company. While this came from a good place - her passion for her business - it meant she often didn't fully get to know the person she was interviewing.

"I think the interview went well," Sarah told Michelle during one of their coaching sessions. "The candidate seemed really interested in the role."

Michelle raised an eyebrow. "That's good, but what did you learn about the candidate?"

Sarah paused, realising she couldn't recall much about the interviewee's background or skills. She had been so focused on selling the role that she had forgotten to assess whether the candidate was actually a good fit.

Michelle explained the importance of a more structured approach to interviewing. "Remember, Sarah, the goal isn't to hire someone just like you. In fact, you often need people with complementary skills and personalities to build a well-rounded team."

Together, they worked on developing a more formalised interview process:

1. **Prepare a standard set of questions**: This ensures consistency across interviews and helps compare candidates objectively.
2. **Use behavioural interview techniques**: Ask candidates to describe how they've handled specific situations in the past, rather than hypothetical scenarios.
3. **Implement skills assessments**: For roles requiring specific technical skills, include a practical component in the interview process.
4. **Involve team members**: Have potential colleagues participate in the interview process to assess team fit.
5. **Use character profiling tools**: Michelle introduced Sarah to tools like DISC (Dominance, Influence, Steadiness, Compliance) assessments to help understand candidates' working styles and personality traits.

Sarah was particularly intrigued by the DISC assessment. "How does this work?" she asked Michelle.

"DISC helps you understand a person's behavioural style," Michelle explained. "For example, someone high in Dominance might be great for a sales role, while someone high in Compliance might excel in a detail-oriented operations position."

Sarah nodded, seeing how this could help her build a more balanced team. She realised she had been unconsciously favouring candidates who were similar to her - high in Influence and Steadiness - when what she really needed was a mix of styles to complement her own strengths and weaknesses.

With this new approach, Sarah's next round of interviews was much more productive. She found herself really listening to candidates, assessing not just their skills but also how they might fit into the team dynamics.

Using these new techniques, Sarah successfully hired an administrative assistant, Emma, and two junior brokers, Tom and Lisa.

The next challenge was learning to delegate effectively.

Michelle: "Remember, Sarah, the goal isn't to create a bunch of mini-Sarahs. It's to build a team where each person's strengths are utilised to create a stronger whole."

Sarah nodded, but still felt hesitant. "I know, but it's hard to let go. What if they make mistakes?"

Michelle smiled understandingly. "That's where your SOPs come in. They provide a framework for consistent quality. And remember, mistakes are opportunities for learning and improvement. Your job now is to lead and mentor, not to do everything yourself."

Over the next few weeks, Sarah practised delegating tasks to her team, using the SOPs as guides. She was pleasantly surprised to find that, with clear procedures in place, her team quickly became proficient in handling many of the day-to-day tasks that had previously consumed her time.

Step 5: Retaining and Motivating Staff

Sarah soon realised that hiring was only half the battle. Retaining and motivating staff was equally important.

Michelle introduced Sarah to some best practices for staff retention and motivation:

1. **Clear communication of expectations**: Use detailed job descriptions and regular performance reviews to ensure everyone understands their role and goals.

2. **Professional development opportunities**: Offer training and support for staff to grow their skills and advance their careers.
3. **Recognition and rewards**: Implement a system to acknowledge and reward good performance, both financially and through non-monetary means.
4. **Work-life balance**: Promote a healthy work-life balance by respecting personal time and offering flexible working arrangements where possible.
5. **Open-door policy**: Encourage staff to share their ideas and concerns freely.
6. **Team building**: Organise regular team activities to foster a sense of community and shared purpose.

Sarah implemented these practices, and over time, she saw a marked improvement in team morale and productivity. Her staff felt valued and invested in the company's success.

To formalise the process of staff development and communication, Michelle introduced Sarah to a structured appraisal format. This would be used in quarterly reviews with each team member:

Sample Staff Development Process

Positioning Statement: "We're going to be doing this once every 3 months, and all I ask is for open and honest dialogue. Between appraisals, if at any time you feel I've been unclear about something, please take responsibility to ask for clarification. It's more likely that I've explained poorly rather than you haven't understood. Also, if at any time you feel you need help, assistance or training, please take responsibility for approaching me and requesting what you need.

If I take responsibility to honour my commitment to your appraisal and asking these 6 questions, and you take responsibility for clarification and assistance between times, then we will always be in a situation where we are both clear on expectations and how to assist where necessary. Is that acceptable to you?"

Question 1 – Where, as a company, are we going? "I'll briefly explain where I feel we are going, but I would love your honesty in where you think we are going as a company and what you would do differently."

Question 2 – Where are you going? "Where do you think you would be best utilised to improve the company's future progress?"

Question 3 – What do you think you are doing well?

Question 4 – If you were your own manager, what suggestions would you be giving yourself to help you improve?

Question 5 – How can I help you make those improvements?

Question 6 – What suggestions and ideas do you have for me to help me improve as your manager?

Closing statement: "Thank you for your time. Can I just ask, what was the biggest takeaway you got from this appraisal?" (Wait for an answer before moving on. Ask for clarification of the answer if required.)

"Don't forget our commitment to each other. I'll take responsibility to honour my commitment to your appraisal and asking these 6 questions, and you take responsibility for clarification and assistance."

Sarah found this structured approach to appraisals transformative. It opened honest dialogues with her team members, helping her understand their perspectives and aspirations while also providing a clear framework for performance improvement and career development.

Step 6: Continuous Improvement

As Sarah's new systems and team settled into place, Michelle introduced the concept of continuous improvement.

Michelle: "Operational excellence isn't a destination, it's a journey. You need to regularly review and refine your processes to stay efficient and adapt to changes in the market."

They established a system for ongoing improvement:

1. Regular Team Feedback: Weekly team meetings where everyone could suggest improvements or report bottlenecks.
2. Client Feedback Collection: A systematic way to gather client feedback after each completed transaction.
3. Quarterly Process Reviews: A thorough review of all SOPs and workflows every three months.
4. Key Performance Indicator (KPI) Tracking: Regular monitoring of metrics like application processing time, client satisfaction scores, and conversion rates.

Sarah embraced this approach, recognising that it would help her business stay agile and responsive to both team and client needs.

The Results of Systemisation

Six months after beginning her operational overhaul, Sarah was amazed at the transformation in her business:

1. Increased Efficiency: What once took her a full day to accomplish, her team now completed in a matter of hours.
2. Improved Client Satisfaction: With more time for meaningful client interactions and consistent follow-ups, Sarah's client satisfaction scores had skyrocketed. Clients appreciated the clear communication and smooth process, often commenting on how much easier it was compared to their previous mortgage experiences.
3. Business Growth: Sarah was able to take on 30% more clients without feeling overwhelmed. The streamlined processes and effective delegation meant that her team could handle a larger volume of applications without sacrificing quality.
4. Better Work-Life Balance: For the first time in years, Sarah felt in control of her schedule and was able to take regular

time off. She no longer felt tethered to her phone 24/7, confident that her team and systems could handle most situations in her absence.

5. Team Empowerment: Her team felt confident and capable, often coming up with innovative ideas to further improve processes. The clear SOPs and regular training sessions meant that everyone understood their role and how it contributed to the larger picture.
6. Financial Improvement: With increased efficiency and capacity, Sarah saw a significant boost in her business's profitability. The initial investment in technology and training had quickly paid for itself.
7. Stronger Lender Relationships: The consistent, high-quality applications submitted by Sarah's team led to stronger relationships with lenders. Some even began to fast-track applications from her brokerage, knowing they could trust the thoroughness of her team's work.

As Sarah wrapped up another smooth, productive day at the office, she couldn't help but feel a sense of pride and accomplishment. She had transformed not just her operations, but her entire approach to her business.

She remembered Michelle's words from their last session: "Sarah, you've done an amazing job. You're no longer just a mortgage broker. You're a business owner and leader. And the best part? You've created a system that delivers consistent, high-quality service to your clients, while giving you the freedom to continue growing and evolving."

Sarah smiled, realising the truth in those words. She had built a business that could run smoothly whether she was in the office or not. She had created repeatable quality through systemisation, just as Michelle had promised.

> *If you were starting your business again tomorrow, who would you not re-employ? For those you named, why are you currently employing them?"*

Challenges and Ongoing Improvements

Despite the overall success, Sarah's journey wasn't without its challenges. As she reflected on the past six months, she identified areas that still needed attention:

1. **Technology Adoption:** While the new CRM system had greatly improved efficiency, some team members were still struggling with certain features. Sarah made a note to schedule additional training sessions and perhaps create more detailed guides for complex processes.
2. **Balancing Systemisation and Personalisation:** Sarah was conscious of the need to maintain a personal touch in client interactions, even as processes became more streamlined. She decided to build in 'personalisation points' in the client journey where team members could add individual flair to communications.
3. **Keeping SOPs Updated:** As regulations in the mortgage industry frequently changed, Sarah realised the importance of regularly updating the SOPs. She assigned team members to be 'owners' of specific SOPs, responsible for keeping them current.
4. **Team Dynamics:** While the DISC assessments had helped in building a diverse team, Sarah noticed some communication challenges between team members with different working styles. She made plans to organise team-building exercises focused on leveraging diverse strengths.
5. **Scalability:** As the business continued to grow, Sarah began to consider how her current systems would scale. Would they still be effective if the team doubled in size? This was a question she planned to explore with Michelle in their next session.

Looking to the Future

As she turned off her computer and prepared to head home, Sarah felt a renewed sense of excitement for the future. She wasn't just working in her business anymore. She was working on it, continuously improving and growing. And that made all the difference.

Sarah began to envision the next phase of her business growth. Perhaps it was time to consider opening a second office in a neighbouring town? Or maybe to expand her services to include commercial mortgages? With her robust operational foundation, these possibilities no longer seemed daunting, but exciting.

She made a mental note to discuss these ideas with her team at their next strategy meeting. Their input had proven invaluable, and Sarah knew that any future growth would be a team effort.

As she locked up the office, Sarah felt a deep sense of gratitude. The journey hadn't been easy, but the rewards - a thriving business, a talented team, satisfied clients, and a balanced life - were well worth the effort.

She stepped out into the evening, looking forward to a relaxing dinner with her family. Tomorrow would bring new challenges and opportunities, but thanks to her streamlined operations and empowered team, Sarah knew she was ready to face whatever came her way.

The transformation was ongoing, but one thing was clear: Sarah was no longer just a mortgage broker. She was a successful business owner, a leader, and an innovator in her field. And she was just getting started.

Team Communication: If you have to deliver the same message more than twice, you don't have a communication problem - you have a documentation problem. Create systems that answer questions before they're asked.

CHAPTER 5 SUMMARY: OPERATIONS - STREAMLINING YOUR BUSINESS

This chapter focused on transforming the operational aspects of a company, emphasising the importance of building repeatable quality through systemisation. Through Sarah's journey, we explored the key elements of streamlined operations:

1. **Process Mapping**: Identifying and visualising current workflows to spot inefficiencies and areas for improvement.
2. **Technology Integration**: Implementing tools like CRM systems, document management software, and digital signature solutions to automate and streamline processes.
3. **Creating Standard Operating Procedures (SOPs)**: Documenting improved workflows to ensure consistency and facilitate training.
4. **Team Building and Delegation**: Hiring and effectively delegating tasks to a capable team, supported by clear SOPs.
5. **Recruiting and Retaining Staff**: Developing a structured interview process, using tools like DISC assessments, and implementing strategies for staff motivation and retention.
6. **Continuous Improvement**: Regularly reviewing and refining processes to maintain efficiency and adapt to changes.

The chapter highlighted how efficient operations can free up a broker's time and energy, allowing for improved client service and business growth. It demonstrated that systemisation, far from being impersonal, actually enables more meaningful client interactions by reducing time spent on administrative tasks.

Key outcomes of Sarah's operational transformation included increased efficiency, improved client satisfaction, business growth, better work-life balance, and team empowerment. The chapter also addressed ongoing challenges and the importance of balancing systemisation with personalisation in client interactions.

Scan here for the WorkBook

WORKSHEETS: IMPLEMENTING OPERATIONAL EXCELLENCE IN YOUR BUSINESS

Worksheet 1: Process Mapping

Objective: Identify inefficiencies and improvement areas in your current processes.

1. List your main business processes (e.g., client onboarding, Lead Pipeline Management, Cash Flow Monitoring and Invoice Tracking, etc.):

   a. ____________________

   b. ____________________

   c. ____________________

2. Choose one process and break it down into steps: Process:

   ____

   Steps:

   a. ____________________

   b. ____________________

   c. ____________________

   (continue as needed)

3. Identify bottlenecks or inefficiencies in this process:

   a. ____________________

   b. ____________________

   c. ____________________

4. Suggest improvements for each inefficiency:

   a. ____________________

   b. ____________________

   c. ____________________

Worksheet 2: Technology Assessment

Objective: Evaluate your current technology and identify areas for improvement.

1. List the software tools you currently use:

   a. ____________________

   b. ____________________

   c. ____________________

2. Identify gaps in your current technology setup:

   a. ____________________

   b. ____________________

   c. ____________________

3. Research potential solutions for each gap:

   Gap a: ____________________ Potential solutions:

   1. ____________________

   2. ____________________

   Gap b: ____________________ Potential solutions:

   1. ____________________

   2. ____________________

4. Prioritise technology improvements:

    1. ______________________________

    2. ______________________________

    3. ______________________________

Worksheet 3: Creating a Standard Operating Procedure (SOP)

Objective: Develop an SOP for a key process in your business.

1. Choose a process: ______________________________
2. Outline the steps:

    a. ______________________________

    b. ______________________________

    c. ______________________________

    (continue as needed)

3. Identify potential issues and solutions:

    Issue 1: ______________________________

    Solution: ______________________________

    Issue 2: ______________________________

    Solution: ______________________________

4. List required resources or tools:

    a. ______________________________

    b. ______________________________

    c. ______________________________

5. Define quality control checkpoints:

   a. ______________________________

   b. ______________________________

   c. ______________________________

Worksheet 4: Recruitment Planning

Objective: Develop a structured approach to recruiting new team members.

1. Identify roles needed in your brokerage:

   a. ______________________________

   b. ______________________________

   c. ______________________________

2. For one role, list key responsibilities:

   Role: ______________________________

   Responsibilities:

   a. ______________________________

   b. ______________________________

   c. ______________________________

3. Develop 5 behavioural interview questions for this role:

   a. ______________________________

   b. ______________________________

   c. ______________________________

   d. ______________________________

   e. ______________________________

4. Define ideal DISC profile for this role:

   Dominance: High / Medium / Low

   Influence: High / Medium / Low

   Steadiness: High / Medium / Low

   Conscientiousness: High / Medium / Low

5. Plan a skills assessment task:

____

____

____

____

Worksheet 5: Staff Retention Strategy

Objective: Develop strategies to motivate and retain your team.

1. List current staff retention challenges:

   a. ____

   b. ____

   c. ____

2. Identify potential professional development opportunities:

   a. ____

   b. ____

   c. ____

3. Design a recognition and reward system:

____

____

4. Plan team building activities:

    a. ______________________________

    b. ______________________________

    c. ______________________________

5. Create an outline for your next team appraisal, using the 6-question format: (Include brief notes on what you hope to achieve with each question)

1. Where, as a company, are we going?

____

____

2. Where are you going?

____

____

3. What do you think you are doing well?

____

____

4. If you were your own manager, what suggestions would you be giving yourself to help you improve?

____

____

5. How can I help you make those improvements?

____

____

6. What suggestions and ideas do you have for me to help me improve as your manager?

____

____

Worksheet 6: Continuous Improvement Plan

Objective: Develop a system for ongoing operational improvement.

1. Set up a schedule for regular process reviews:

____

____

2. Identify Key Performance Indicators (KPIs) to track:

   a. ____________________________________

   b. ____________________________________

   c. ____________________________________

3. Design a system for collecting team feedback:

____

____

4. Create a client feedback survey: (List 5 key questions)

   a. ____________________________________

   b. ____________________________________

   c. ____________________________________

   d. ____________________________________

   e. ____________________________________

5. Schedule your next operational review:

   Date: ______________________________

   Key areas to focus on:

   a. ______________________________

   b. ______________________________

   c. ______________________________

Remember, operational excellence is an ongoing journey. Regularly revisit these worksheets and adjust your strategies as your business grows and evolves. By continuously refining your processes, leveraging technology, and developing your team, you'll build a more efficient, scalable, and successful company.

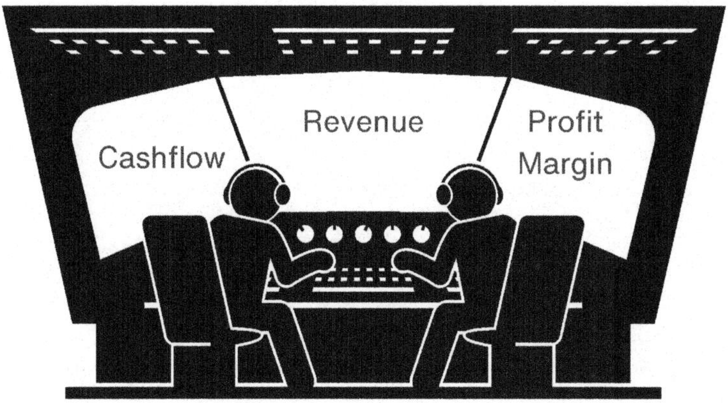
Revenue
Profit
Margin
Cashflow

CHAPTER 6: FINANCE - MANAGING THE LIFEBLOOD OF YOUR BUSINESS

"Money, like emotions, is something you must control to keep your life on the right track."
– Natasha Munson

Revenue Focus: The numbers you track are the numbers that grow. If you obsess over social media followers, you'll get followers. If you obsess over profit margins, you'll get profit. Choose your metrics carefully - they shape behaviour.

Sarah leaned back in her chair; her eyes fixed on the monitor before her. The spreadsheet displayed wasn't just a collection of numbers; it was the story of her business, laid bare in rows and columns. For the first time since she'd started her brokerage, she felt a true sense of financial clarity.

The journey to this point hadn't been easy. Sarah remembered the overwhelming feeling of dread that used to accompany any thought of her business finances. The shoebox full of receipts, the vague idea of profitability based solely on her bank balance - it all seemed like a distant memory now.

With a click, she switched to her newly implemented financial dashboard. Here, in real-time, she could see her revenue streams, expenses, profitability ratios, and cash flow projections. The graph showing her monthly revenue trend brought a smile to her face - the upward trajectory was unmistakable.

Her gaze lingered on the cash flow forecast. There was a potential dip coming in three months, coinciding with the typically slower summer period. But unlike in previous years, this didn't spark panic. Instead, Sarah felt a sense of control. She had seen this coming and had already begun implementing strategies to mitigate the impact.

A notification popped up on her screen - a reminder of her quarterly meeting with her accountant later that day. Sarah felt a surge of confidence. For the first time, she was looking forward to this meeting, eager to discuss tax planning strategies and explore options for reinvesting in her growing business.

As she closed the spreadsheet, Sarah reflected on how this newfound financial acumen had transformed not just her business, but her entire approach to being a mortgage broker. She was no longer just reacting to the market; she was planning for the future, making informed decisions, and building a truly sustainable business.

The Journey to Financial Clarity

Sarah's transformation didn't happen overnight. It began with a conversation with her mentor, Michelle, who helped her understand that financial management wasn't just about keeping the taxman happy - it was about steering her business towards success.

(Flashback to Sarah's session with Michelle)

Sarah: "Michelle, I have to admit, I'm terrified of the financial side of my business. Numbers have never been my strong suit."

Michelle smiled understandingly. "Sarah, think of your business finances like a navigation system for your car. Without it, you might still reach your destination, but you'll probably take some wrong turns, waste time and fuel, and feel stressed throughout the journey. With it, you can see where you are, plan your route, and adjust if you encounter obstacles."

Sarah nodded slowly, beginning to see the analogy. "So, where do I start?"

Michelle pulled out a notebook. "Let's begin with the basics. We'll break it down into simple steps that anyone can follow, even a teenager managing their pocket money. Then we'll build from there."

> *Investment Strategy: The best time to make major business investments is when your competitors are fearful. During market downturns, talent is more available, advertising is cheaper, and opportunities are overlooked by others playing it safe.*

Finance 101: The Basics

Michelle began by explaining the three fundamental financial statements every business owner should understand:

1. **Income Statement (Profit and Loss Statement)**: "Think of this as your business's report card," Michelle explained. "It shows how much money you're making (revenue), how much you're spending (expenses), and what's left over (profit) over a specific period."
2. **Balance Sheet**: "This is like a snapshot of your business's financial health at a specific moment. It shows what you own (assets), what you owe (liabilities), and the difference between them (equity)."
3. **Cash Flow Statement**: "This tracks the actual money moving in and out of your business. Remember, profit doesn't always equal cash - you might make a sale today but not get paid for 3-months."

Sarah's head was spinning, but Michelle assured her they would tackle each concept one at a time.

Understanding Revenue and Expenses

Michelle started with the basics of the Income Statement.

"Let's break down your business's money into two simple categories: money coming in (revenue) and money going out (expenses)," Michelle said.

Together, they listed out Sarah's revenue sources:

- Commissions from completed mortgages
- Broker fees
- Fees for additional services & referrals

Then, they categorised her expenses:

- Office rent
- Utilities
- Salaries (including Sarah's own draw)
- Marketing costs
- Software subscriptions
- Professional fees (accountant, lawyer)
- Training and development

Michelle explained, "The goal is to have more money coming in than going out. That's your profit. But it's not just about the bottom line - understanding where your money comes from and where it goes helps you make better decisions."

Cashflow: The Lifeblood of Your Business

"Now," Michelle continued, "let's talk about cashflow. This is crucial because you can be profitable on paper but still run out of cash if you're not careful."

Michelle opened a simple Excel spreadsheet and showed Sarah how to create a basic cashflow forecast:

1. Across the top, she listed the months of the year.
2. Down the left side, she listed Sarah's regular operating costs.
3. Below the operating costs, she created a space to enter client names and expected commission amounts.

"Here's how it works," Michelle explained. "You enter your expected commissions in the month you expect to receive them. The spreadsheet will automatically subtract your operating costs. If you're short for the month, it'll show in red. As you add more expected income, it'll turn green once you've hit your break-even point."

Sarah watched in amazement as Michelle demonstrated, entering some sample figures. The simplicity and visual nature of the spreadsheet made the concept of cashflow suddenly clear.

"This is incredible," Sarah breathed. "I can actually see when I might have cash shortages and plan for them."

Michelle nodded. "Exactly. And as you get more sophisticated, you can add more details, like separating fixed and variable costs, or factoring in tax payments."

Profitability Ratios: Measuring Your Business's Health

As Sarah grew more comfortable with the basics, Michelle introduced some simple profitability ratios.

1. **Gross Profit Margin**: "This shows how much money you keep from each sale after direct costs. For a mortgage broker, this might be your commission minus any referral fees you pay out."

   Calculation: (Revenue - Direct Costs) / Revenue x 100

2. **Net Profit Margin**: "This is the percentage of revenue that turns into profit after all expenses are paid."

   Calculation: Net Profit / Revenue x 100

3. **Break-Even Point**: "This is how much revenue you need to cover all your costs. It's crucial for planning."

   Calculation: Fixed Costs / (1 - Variable Costs Percentage)

Michelle helped Sarah calculate these for her business, explaining what each number meant and how to use them to make decisions.

Creating a Financial Dashboard

With a grasp of the basics, Michelle helped Sarah create a simple one-page financial dashboard. They chose key metrics that would give Sarah a quick overview of her business's financial health:

1. Monthly Revenue
2. Gross Profit Margin
3. Net Profit Margin
4. Cash Balance
5. Upcoming Expenses (next 30 days)
6. Pipeline Value (potential commissions from in-progress applications)

"Check this daily," Michelle advised. "It'll help you keep your finger on the pulse of your business without getting bogged down in details.

It's also worth adding a few extra measures such as leads & first appointment completed & second appointment completed. Knowing these can help flag potential concerns. If you know leads are down, then you need to look at your marketing. If the appointments being sat are down then, is it lead quality or is it the advisors need further sales training. Having this as an early warning system really helps, especially in the Mortgage industry as there's often a four-month gap between submitting an application and receiving payment. Waiting to see a drop in revenue before acting is often too late.

Tax Planning and Compliance

As Sarah's financial acumen grew, Michelle stressed the importance of proper tax planning and compliance.

"Tax isn't just about filling out forms once a year," Michelle explained. "With proper planning, you can often reduce your tax bill legally and ethically."

They discussed strategies like:

- Timing of expenses and income
- Maximising allowable deductions
- Setting aside money for tax payments
- The importance of accurate record-keeping

Michelle also introduced Sarah to the concept of working with a professional accountant. "Think of it as an investment," she said. "A good accountant can often save you more than they cost."

Investing in Growth

As Sarah's business became more financially stable, Michelle introduced the concept of reinvesting profits for growth.

"Now that you understand your finances, you can make informed decisions about investing in your business," Michelle explained. "This might mean hiring new staff, upgrading your technology, or expanding your marketing efforts."

They worked on creating a simple return on investment (ROI) calculator to help Sarah evaluate potential investments.

The Result: Financial Confidence

Months later, Sarah sat across from her accountant, Alex, feeling a new sense of confidence.

Sarah: "Thanks for meeting with me, Alex. I'm excited to go over our quarterly financials."

Alex (Accountant): "It's my pleasure, Sarah. I have to say, the level of detail and organisation in your financial records is impressive. It makes my job much easier."

Sarah: "That means a lot, coming from you. I've been working hard to get a handle on our finances. Can we start by looking at our profitability ratios?"

Alex: "Absolutely. Your gross profit margin has increased by 5% compared to last quarter, which is excellent. However, I noticed your operating expenses have also gone up slightly."

Sarah: "Yes, that's due to the new CRM system we implemented. I'm hoping it will lead to increased efficiency and sales in the long run."

Alex: "That's a sound investment. Now, let's talk about your tax situation. Given your projected income for the year, we might want to consider..."

The conversation continued, touching on tax planning, cash flow management, and strategies for reinvesting profits. Sarah found herself actively engaged, asking informed questions and confidently discussing financial concepts that would have baffled her just months ago.

As she left the meeting, Sarah reflected on her journey. She had gone from fearing finances to embracing them as a powerful tool for growing her business. She wasn't just a mortgage broker anymore - she was a savvy business owner, using financial insights to steer her brokerage towards a prosperous future.

CHAPTER 6 SUMMARY: FINANCE - MANAGING THE LIFEBLOOD OF YOUR BUSINESS

This chapter focused on demystifying financial management for mortgage brokers, emphasising its critical role in running a successful brokerage. Through Sarah's journey, we explored key financial concepts and strategies:

1. **Basic Financial Statements**: Understanding the Income Statement, Balance Sheet, and Cash Flow Statement.
2. **Revenue and Expenses**: Identifying and categorising money coming in and going out of the business.
3. **Cashflow Management**: Using a simple Excel-based system to forecast and monitor cash flow.
4. **Profitability Ratios**: Learning to calculate and interpret basic financial ratios.
5. **Financial Dashboard**: Creating a one-page overview of key financial metrics.
6. **Tax Planning and Compliance**: Understanding the importance of proper tax management.
7. **Investing in Growth**: Making informed decisions about reinvesting profits.

The chapter highlighted how solid financial management can provide clarity, reduce stress, and create opportunities for growth. It emphasised that financial acumen is a skill that can be learned and improved over time.

Scan here for the WorkBook

FINANCE MODULE WORKBOOK

Exercise 1: Understanding Your Revenue and Expenses

1. List all your sources of revenue:

   a. ______________________________

   b. ______________________________

   c. ______________________________

2. List and categorize your main expenses: Fixed Expenses:

   a. ______________________________

   b. ______________________________

   c. ______________________________

   Variable Expenses:

   a. ______________________________

   b. ______________________________

   c. ______________________________

Exercise 2: Creating a Simple Cash Flow Forecast

Using Excel or a similar spreadsheet program, create a 6-month cash flow forecast:

1. List months across the top row.
2. List your operating costs down the left column.
3. Create a space below operating costs to enter client names and expected commissions.

4. Use a simple formula to calculate the difference between expected income and expenses for each month.
5. Use conditional formatting to show shortfalls in red and surpluses in green.

After creating your spreadsheet, answer the following:

1. In which month(s) do you anticipate cash flow challenges?

____

____

2. What strategies could you implement to address these challenges?

____

____

Simple Cash Flow Forecast Spreadsheet

Here's a representation of the Excel spreadsheet for cash flow forecasting. In an actual Excel file, you would use formulas to calculate totals and apply conditional formatting for color-coding.

Item	Written	January	February	March	April	May	June
Operating Costs							
Office Rent		£1,500	£1,500	£1,500	£1,500	£1,500	£1,500
Utilities		£200	£200	£200	£200	£200	£200
Salaries		£5,000	£5,000	£5,000	£5,000	£5,000	£5,000
Marketing		£1,500	£1,500	£1,500	£1,500	£1,500	£1,500
Software Subs		£500	£500	£500	£500	£500	£500
Other Expences		£600	£600	£600	£600	£600	£600
Total Expences		£9,300	£9,300	£9,300	£9,300	£9,300	£9,300
Smith Fee	October	Paid					
Smith Mortgage	October	£1,200					
Smith Life	October	£2,200					
Jones Fee	October	Paid					
Jones Mortgage	October	£960					
Burton fee	October	Paid					
Burton Mortgage	October	£875					
Burton Life	October	£1,550					
Jackson Fee	October	Paid					
Jackson Mortgage	October	£1,400					
Jackson Life	October	£1,800					
Jennings Comm	October		£6,400				
Turner fee	October	Paid					
Turner Mortgage	November		£980				
Turner Life	October		£2,250				
Total Income		£9,985	£9,630	£0	£0	£0	£0
Total Expences		£9,300	£9,300	£9,300	£9,300	£9,300	£9,300
Profit / Loss		£685	£330	**£9,300**	**£9,300**	**£9,300**	**£9,300**

In Excel, you would:

1. Use formulas to calculate the Total Expenses, Total Income, Net Cash Flow, and Cumulative Cash Flow rows.
2. Apply conditional formatting to the Net Cash Flow row:
    - If the value is negative, format the cell background to red
    - If the value is positive, format the cell background to green
3. As you add more expected income throughout the month, the colours will change, giving you a visual representation of your cash flow status.

Instructions for use:

4. Update the Operating Costs section with your actual fixed and estimated variable costs.
5. As you secure new clients or receive confirmations of upcoming commissions, add them to the Expected Income section in the month you expect to receive the payment.
6. Regularly review your Net Cash Flow and Cumulative Cash Flow to identify potential cash flow issues in advance.
7. Use this forecast to make informed decisions about expenses, marketing efforts, and when you might need to secure additional funding or focus on bringing in more business.

Remember, this is a basic template. As you become more comfortable with financial forecasting, you can expand this spreadsheet to include more detailed categories, separate sheets for different scenarios, or even link it to your actual accounting software for more accurate projections.

Exercise 3: Calculating Basic Profitability Ratios

Using your financial data from the last quarter, calculate the following:

1. Gross Profit Margin: (Revenue - Direct Costs) / Revenue x 100 = _______%
2. Net Profit Margin: Net Profit / Revenue x 100 = _______%
3. Break-Even Point: Fixed Costs / (1 - Variable Costs Percentage) = £_______

What do these numbers tell you about your business's financial health?

____

____

Exercise 4: Creating Your Financial Dashboard

Design a one-page financial dashboard for your brokerage. List the 5-7 most important metrics you want to track regularly:

1. ______________________________
2. ______________________________
3. ______________________________
4. ______________________________
5. ______________________________
6. ______________________________
7. ______________________________

How often will you update and review this dashboard? ________

Exercise 5: Tax Planning

1. List three strategies you can implement for better tax management:

    a. ______________________________

    b. ______________________________

    c. ______________________________

2. When was your last meeting with a professional accountant?

____

____

3. Schedule your next meeting:

____

____

Exercise 6: Investing in Growth

Identify three potential areas for reinvestment in your business:

1. ______________________________

Estimated Cost: £________

Expected Benefit: ______________________

2. ______________________________

Estimated Cost: £________

Expected Benefit: ______________________

3. ______________________________

Estimated Cost: £________

Expected Benefit: ______________________

Action Plan

Based on what you've learned in this chapter, list three immediate actions you will take to improve your brokerage's financial management:

1. ______________________________
2. ______________________________
3. ______________________________

Remember, becoming financially savvy is a journey. Regularly revisit these exercises and continually educate yourself on financial matters. By maintaining a clear understanding of your business's finances, you'll be better equipped to make informed decisions and drive your brokerage towards sustainable growth.

FINAL CHAPTER: THE SUMMIT OF SUCCESS - YOUR INTEGRATED COMPANY

"To be successful, you have to have your heart in your business and your business in your heart."
– Tony Hsieh

Sarah stood at the large window of her office, gazing out at the bustling city below. The view from the 15th floor was breathtaking, but it wasn't the scenery that had her attention. She was lost in thought, reflecting on the incredible journey that had brought her and her business to this point.

It had been five years since she'd embarked on her transformation journey, guided by the Four Pillars approach. Now, at 37, Sarah found herself at a crossroads she'd never imagined reaching so soon.

The Four Pillars in Action

A gentle knock at the door interrupted her reverie. "Come in," she called, turning from the window.

Emma, her operations manager and now general manager, entered with a tablet in hand. "Sarah, I've got the latest reports ready for your review. And... there's something else we need to discuss."

Sarah smiled, gesturing for Emma to take a seat. "Let's start with the reports. How are we looking?"

Emma's face lit up as she began to run through the numbers. "It's all good news. Our client acquisition cost is down 15% from last quarter, while our average client lifetime value has increased by 20%. Our marketing efficiency ratio is at an all-time high - we're getting £5.50 back for every pound spent on marketing."

Sarah nodded, unsurprised but pleased. The marketing pillar of her business had come a long way from the days of haphazard efforts and unmeasured results. She remembered the turning point when they had implemented a comprehensive digital marketing strategy, complete with targeted content marketing, social media campaigns, and a robust CRM system to track every interaction.

"Tell me more about the marketing campaigns," Sarah prompted. "Which ones are performing best?"

Emma swiped through her tablet. "Our 'First-Time Buyer's Guide' series on social media has been a huge hit. It's generated a 40% increase in inquiries from that demographic. The automated email nurture campaign for past clients has also been successful - we've seen a 25% uptick in referrals."

Sarah smiled, remembering the days when she used to worry about where the next client would come from. Now, their marketing machine ran smoothly, consistently bringing in a stream of qualified leads.

"And how about our sales performance?" Sarah asked, moving on to the second pillar.

Emma's grin widened. "Our conversion rate has improved by 10% this quarter. The new consultative selling approach you implemented has really paid off. Clients are responding well to our more personalised, education-focused process."

Sarah nodded, recalling the resistance she'd initially faced when introducing the new sales methodology. It had taken time and training, but the results spoke for themselves. Their team of mortgage advisors now operated more like financial educators than traditional salespeople, building trust and long-term relationships with clients.

"Can you give me an example of a particularly successful case?" Sarah asked.

Emma nodded enthusiastically. "Just last week, Tom worked with a couple who came in thinking they couldn't afford to buy. Through our detailed affordability assessment and by exploring various mortgage products, he was able to find a solution that worked for them. They're now on track to buy their first home, and they've already referred three friends to us."

Sarah felt a surge of pride. This was why she'd gotten into the mortgage business in the first place - to help people achieve their dreams of homeownership.

"That's fantastic," Sarah said. "Now, what about our operations? How are we handling the increased volume?"

Emma switched to another screen on her tablet. "Our streamlined processes are holding up well. The automated workflow system we implemented last year has increased our efficiency by 30%. We're processing applications faster than ever, with fewer errors."

Sarah remembered the chaos of their old paper-based system, with files piling up on desks and important documents occasionally going missing. The transition to a fully digital, automated system had been challenging, but the results were undeniable.

"And our team capacity?" Sarah inquired.

"Our advisors are operating at 85% capacity, which is right in our optimal zone. The admin team is handling the current volume comfortably, with room to support a 30% increase in business without additional hires."

Sarah nodded approvingly. They had worked hard to find the right balance - keeping the team busy enough to be productive, but not so overwhelmed that quality suffered.

"Excellent," Sarah said. "Now, let's talk about the financial picture."

Emma pulled up the financial dashboard. "We're in a strong position. Revenue is up 25% year-on-year, and our profit margin has increased from 15% to 22%. The cost-cutting measures we implemented in non-core areas have paid off, and our investments in technology are showing a solid return."

Sarah leaned back in her chair, taking in the numbers. The financial pillar had always been her weak spot in the early days, but now it was a source of strength and clarity. Regular financial reviews, clear budgeting processes, and data-driven decision-making had transformed their financial management.

"What about our cash flow projection for the next quarter?" Sarah asked.

Emma pulled up another chart. "We're looking strong. Even with the planned investment in the new client portal, we're projecting a healthy positive cash flow. Our improved invoicing system and the shift to monthly retainer fees for some of our high-net-worth clients have really stabilised our cash flow."

Sarah nodded, remembering the days of feast-or-famine that used to characterise their finances. The move to more predictable revenue streams had been a game-changer.

"Thank you, Emma. This all looks excellent," Sarah said. "Now, what was the other thing you wanted to discuss?"

Emma hesitated for a moment, then took a deep breath. "We've received another acquisition offer. It's from DeVere Group. They're offering £3.5 million for the business."

Sarah's breath caught in her throat. It wasn't the first offer they'd received - over the past year, several independent financial advisory firms had approached them. But this was by far the most substantial offer yet.

As Emma continued to explain the details of the offer, Sarah's mind drifted back to one of her earliest meetings with Michelle, her business coach. Michelle's words echoed in her memory:

"Whatever your initial plans are for Harmony Mortgages, we must build as if we intend to sell. That way we'll always remain focused on systems and processes."

At the time, Sarah had been surprised by this advice. Selling her business had been the furthest thing from her mind. But now, she realised how prescient Michelle's words had been. It was precisely because they had built the business with such robust systems and processes that they were now able to consider this offer.

The Culmination of Success

"They're impressed by our metrics," Emma continued. "Our clear processes, our measurable outcomes, our growth trajectory - they see us as a turnkey operation that could slot right into their existing structure."

Sarah nodded slowly, her mind racing. "I see. Can you send me the details? I'll need some time to think this over."

After Emma left, Sarah returned to the window, her reflection of the past now tinged with thoughts of the future. The business was running like a well-oiled machine, largely without her day-to-day involvement as a business owner and with no involvement as a Mortgage Advisor, having surrendered her FCA licence just over 12 months ago. She had a clear dashboard of key performance indicators that gave her instant insight into every aspect of the operation. The four pillars - Marketing, Sales, Operations, and Finance - were not just concepts anymore, but the very foundation of their success.

She thought back to the chaos of her early days as a broker. The shoebox of receipts, the missed follow-ups, the feast-or-famine cycle of clients. Now, everything was measured, optimised, and integrated. They knew exactly how much it cost to acquire a client, the lifetime value of each client relationship, the precise capacity of their team, and the return on every pound spent. And all this with minimal involvement from Sarah.

This level of clarity and control had allowed them to scale rapidly while maintaining quality. It had also made the business incredibly attractive to potential buyers.

Sarah's phone buzzed with a calendar reminder. It was time for the weekly strategy meeting. As she walked to the conference room, she marvelled at how different these meetings were now compared to the early days.

The Strategy Meeting

"Good afternoon, everyone," Sarah said as she entered the room. Her leadership team – Emma & the heads of Marketing, Sales, and Finance - were already seated.

"Today, I want to discuss our plans for the next quarter, but first, I have some news to share." Sarah paused, looking around the table. "We've received another acquisition offer. This one is significant - £3.5 million from the DeVere Group."

A mix of excitement and concern flashed across the faces around the table.

"I haven't made any decisions yet," Sarah continued. "But I want us to discuss this openly. Our success has made us a very attractive prospect, and I need to consider all options for the future of the business."

Mark, the head of marketing, spoke up first. "From a marketing perspective, we're just hitting our stride. Our brand recognition is growing, and we're seeing increased engagement across all channels. Being part of a larger organisation could give us access to more resources, but it might also dilute our unique identity."

Sarah nodded, appreciating Mark's insight. "Good point. Lisa, what's your take from the sales side?"

Lisa, the sales director, leaned forward. "Our team has really embraced the consultative selling approach. We're not just closing deals; we're building long-term relationships. My concern would be whether DeVere would maintain this approach or push for more aggressive sales tactics."

"Valid concern," Sarah agreed. "Emma, you've seen the offer. What's your perspective on how it would affect our operations?"

Emma took a moment before responding. "Our operational efficiency is one of our biggest strengths. DeVere seems to recognise this, which is why they're interested. However, integrating with their systems could be challenging. We'd need to ensure our processes aren't compromised."

Finally, Sarah turned to David, the finance director. "David, what are your thoughts from a financial standpoint?"

David adjusted his glasses. "The offer is certainly attractive. It represents a significant premium on our current valuation. However, given our growth trajectory and improving margins, we could potentially be worth even more in a year or two if we continue on this path."

Sarah absorbed all their input, feeling grateful for the talented team she had built. "Thank you all for your insights. This is exactly why we're successful - because we consider all aspects of the business in our decision-making."

She paused, gathering her thoughts. "Now, let's talk about our plans for the next quarter. Regardless of any potential sale, we need to keep pushing forward. Mark, what's on the horizon for marketing?"

Mark pulled up a presentation on the screen. "We're planning to launch a new video series called 'Mortgage Myths Debunked.' It's designed to address common misconceptions about mortgages and position us as trusted educators in the field. We're also expanding our partnerships with local estate agencies to increase our referral network. What's interesting is that these agents are approaching us to work with them and are happy to accept a lower fee than normal. It seems that they understand how powerful our conversion rate is which would actually lead them to greater income than going with a lesser broker offering a higher fee"

Sarah nodded approvingly. "Excellent. This aligns perfectly with our mission to educate and empower our clients. Lisa, how will sales support this initiative?"

Lisa jumped in, "We're developing a new training program for our advisors to enhance their skills in addressing these common myths during client consultations. We're also creating a series of webinars that align with the video content, allowing us to engage directly with potential clients and showcase our expertise."

"Great synergy between marketing and sales," Sarah commented. "Emma, how are our operations set up to handle the potential increase in inquiries and clients?"

Emma pulled up a flowchart on her tablet. "We've optimised our CRM to automatically categorise and prioritise leads coming in from these new initiatives. We've also enhanced our onboarding process to ensure new clients are guided smoothly through each stage of the mortgage journey."

Sarah smiled, seeing how seamlessly the different aspects of the business were working together. "And David, how does this all look from a financial perspective?"

David referred to his notes. "We've run the numbers, and the projected ROI on these initiatives is strong. We've allocated budget from our marketing fund to support the video series and webinars. Based on our conversion rates and average client value, we're expecting these efforts to boost our revenue by 15% in the coming quarter."

As the meeting continued, Sarah felt a deep sense of pride and accomplishment. This is what she had always envisioned - a company that operated with the precision of a Swiss watch, each part working in harmony with the others.

The Decision-Making Process

Over the next few weeks, Sarah engaged in deep discussions with her mentors, her family, and her team. She pored over the business metrics, considering various future scenarios. The numbers told a story of a business primed for continued success, but they also highlighted the incredible value they had built - value that could open new opportunities if realised.

She scheduled a series of meetings with the DeVere team, diving deep into their vision for the merged company. She was impressed by their strategic thinking but also wary of how her team and clients might be affected by such a significant change.

During one particularly late night at the office, Sarah found herself creating a pros and cons list:

Pros of Selling:

1. Significant personal financial gain
2. Access to greater resources for growth
3. Potential for wider impact in the industry
4. Reduced personal stress and responsibility
5. New challenges and learning opportunities

Cons of Selling:

1. Loss of full control over the business
2. Potential changes to company culture
3. Uncertainty for team members
4. Risk of losing the personal touch with clients
5. Emotional challenge of letting go

As she stared at the list, Sarah realised that the decision wasn't just about numbers. It was about the future she envisioned for herself, her team, and the clients they served.

She thought back to the day she had started her brokerage, working from a tiny office with just a desk and a dream. The journey had been challenging, often exhausting, but incredibly rewarding. She had not only built a successful business but had also grown as a leader and a person.

The Four Pillars approach had transformed her business, but it had also transformed her. She was no longer a mortgage broker; she was a strategic thinker, a team builder, a financial expert, and a visionary leader.

As she mulled over the decision, Sarah realised that the very systems and processes she had put in place were what made this choice possible. The business could run smoothly without her constant involvement, which opened a world of possibilities.

The Final Decision

Three months after receiving the offer, Sarah found herself sitting in a lawyer's office, pen in hand. After much deliberation, she had decided to accept the DeVere Group's offer. The contract before her represented not just a significant personal windfall, but a promise to her team and her clients that the business she had built would continue to thrive and grow. She'd also managed to negotiate an extremely healthy "signing on bonus" for her management team when they transferred to DeVere.

As she signed her name, Sarah felt a mix of emotions - pride in what she had accomplished, gratitude for the journey, and excitement for the future. But she also felt a twinge of apprehension about the process that lay ahead.

The Post-Acceptance Process

Sarah quickly learned that signing the contract was just the beginning of a complex and sometimes challenging process.

Due Diligence: In the weeks following the acceptance of the offer, DeVere Group's team of accountants, lawyers, and business analysts descended on Harmony Mortgages. They meticulously examined every aspect of the business - financial records, client files, operational processes, and more. Sarah was grateful for the robust systems they had put in place; it made the due diligence process much smoother than it might have been otherwise.

There were still stressful moments, like when the DeVere team questioned a dip in sales from two years ago. Sarah was able to explain that it coincided with a regulatory change in the mortgage industry and showed how they had quickly adapted their processes to recover and exceed their previous performance.

Transition Planning: As part of the deal, Sarah had agreed to stay on with the company for 12 months to manage the handover. This period would be crucial for ensuring a smooth transition and maintaining the trust of clients and employees.

Together with the DeVere Group management team, Sarah developed a comprehensive transition plan. This included:

1. A communication strategy for informing clients about the change in ownership
2. A series of training sessions to familiarise DeVere staff with Harmony's unique processes and systems
3. A plan for gradually transferring Sarah's responsibilities to other team members

Sarah found this process both challenging and rewarding. It was difficult to let go of the reins, but she also felt a sense of pride in seeing her team step up to take on more responsibility.

Integration Challenges: Despite careful planning, there were inevitably some bumps in the road. Some of Harmony's long-standing clients were initially wary of the change in ownership. Sarah spent countless hours on the phone, reassuring them that the level of service they had come to expect would not change.

There were also some cultural clashes between Harmony's close-knit team and DeVere's more corporate environment. Sarah found herself playing the role of mediator, helping both sides understand and appreciate each other's perspectives.

Looking to the Future: As the months passed, Sarah began to see the benefits of the acquisition. Harmony now had access to resources that allowed them to expand their services and reach even more clients. The DeVere Group, in turn, was implementing some of Harmony's innovative processes across their other divisions.

Sarah also started to think about her own future. With the business in good hands, she found herself excited about new possibilities. She had always been passionate about financial education, and now she was considering starting a non-profit focused on improving financial literacy among young adults.

As her 12-month transition period neared its end, Sarah felt a complex mix of emotions. There was sadness at the thought of leaving the business she had built, but also excitement for the future. Most of all, there was a deep sense of satisfaction. She had built something of real value - not just in financial terms, but in the impact, it had made on clients' lives and the opportunities it had created for her team.

Sarah knew that whatever came next, the lessons she had learned through building and selling Harmony Mortgages would serve her well. The Four Pillars approach hadn't just built a successful business; it had shaped her into a leader ready for new challenges.

Reflecting on the Journey

As the transition period neared its end, Sarah spent a day walking through the office, taking it all in one last time as the owner. She stopped at each department, reflecting on how far they had come.

In the marketing department, she saw the content calendar for the next 12 months pinned to the wall, a far cry from the ad-hoc approach of the early days. The sales team were engaged in a training session, role-playing complex client scenarios and discussing ethical approaches to challenging situations. In operations, she observed the quiet efficiency of a well-oiled machine, with the team seamlessly managing a high volume of applications. And in the finance department, she noted with pride the array of dashboards displaying real-time metrics on everything from cash flow to client acquisition costs.

Each area of the business was strong in its own right, but what truly set them apart was how these pillars worked together. Marketing efforts seamlessly fed into the sales process. Sales insights informed operational improvements. Operational efficiencies boosted financial performance. And financial data guided marketing investments. It was a virtuous cycle that had propelled them to heights Sarah had once only dreamed of.

As she prepared to leave the office for the last time, Sarah was struck by a realisation. The true value of what she had built wasn't just in the impressive metrics or the sales price. It was in the lives touched - the first-time homebuyers they'd guided, the families they'd helped refinance to better terms, the investors they'd supported in growing their portfolios. It was in the team she'd developed, watching individuals grow into confident professionals.

The Next Chapter

Nine months later...

The warm Caribbean breeze ruffled Sarah's hair as she sat on the pristine white sand, watching her children play in the gentle waves. The beachfront villa they had rented for six weeks stretched out behind her, a luxurious base for their extended family holiday.

Sarah picked up her tablet, smiling as she reviewed the latest report from her old business. The transition to new ownership had been smooth, and the systems and processes she had put in place continued to drive success. Her team, now with additional resources from DeVere, were achieving new heights.

The marketing department had expanded its reach, launching a popular podcast about homeownership and financial literacy. Sales had increased by 30% in the first two quarters after the acquisition, a testament to the scalability of the systems she had put in place. The operations team had successfully integrated with DeVere's larger infrastructure, maintaining efficiency while handling a significantly larger volume of applications. And financially, the business was outperforming even the most optimistic projections from the acquisition plan.

As she set the tablet aside, Sarah's mind drifted to the future. The sale of her business had opened a world of possibilities. She had time, financial freedom, and a wealth of knowledge and experience to draw upon.

Several ideas had been percolating in her mind:

1. **Consulting Firm**: Leveraging her experience to help other small business owners implement the Four Pillars approach. She envisioned working with entrepreneurs across various industries, showing them how integrated, measurable business practices could transform their operations.
2. **Tech Startup**: Developing software that could help businesses achieve the level of measurability and integration she had created in her brokerage. She imagined a platform that could provide real-time insights across all four pillars, making data-driven decision-making accessible to businesses of all sizes.
3. **Education Initiative**: Creating a comprehensive program to improve financial literacy, especially around homeownership and mortgages. She saw an opportunity to make a broader impact, helping people understand and navigate the often-complex world of personal finance.

4. **Impact Investing**: Using her financial resources to support and grow ethical businesses. She was particularly interested in fintech startups aimed at making financial services more accessible and transparent.
5. **Writing a Book**: Sharing her journey and the lessons learned, providing a roadmap for other entrepreneurs to build sustainable, successful businesses.

Each of these possibilities excited her in different ways, but for now, they could wait. Sarah leaned back in her beach chair, feeling the warm sun on her face. She had learned the importance of balance, of stepping back to gain perspective. This time with her family was precious, a chance to recharge and reflect.

As she watched her children's laughter carried on the sea breeze, Sarah felt a deep sense of contentment. The journey of building her business had been challenging, often stressful, but ultimately incredibly rewarding. She had not just created a successful company, but had grown as a person, a leader, and a visionary.

The Lasting Impact of the Four Pillars

As Sarah reflected on her journey, she realised that the Four Pillars approach had become more than just a business strategy. It had evolved into a philosophy that could be applied to various aspects of life:

1. **Marketing** had taught her the importance of clear communication and understanding one's audience, skills that were valuable in all relationships.
2. **Sales** had shown her the power of empathy and active listening, enhancing her ability to connect with people from all walks of life.
3. **Operations** had instilled in her a love for efficiency and continuous improvement, approaches she now applied to personal projects and family life.
4. **Finance** had given her a framework for making informed decisions, whether in business or personal matters.

The integration of these pillars - the way they supported and enhanced each other - had demonstrated the power of a holistic, balanced approach to any challenge.

Sarah smiled, her mind already starting to sketch out plans for her next venture. But those plans could wait, at least for a little while longer. Right now, she had a sandcastle to build with her children.

As she stood up and walked towards the water's edge, Sarah felt a sense of excitement for the future. Whatever path she chose next, she knew she had the tools, the experience, and the mindset to make it a success.

The sun was setting over the Caribbean Sea, painting the sky in brilliant hues of orange and pink. Sarah took a deep breath, savouring the moment. She had climbed to the summit of success in her company business, but she realised now that it wasn't the end of her journey. It was just the beginning of a new adventure.

The Four Pillars that had transformed her business would now guide her into this next chapter of her life. As she joined her family at the water's edge, laughing as the warm waves lapped at her feet, Sarah knew that the best was yet to come.

EPILOGUE: THE RIPPLE EFFECT

Five years after the sale of her company, Sarah stood at a podium, addressing a packed auditorium. She had just finished giving a keynote speech at a major business conference, sharing her journey and the principles that had guided her success.

"The Four Pillars approach isn't just about building a successful business," she concluded. "It's about creating value, fostering growth, and making a positive impact. Whether you're running a company, a tech startup, or a local coffee shop, these principles can transform your business and your life."

As applause filled the room, Sarah felt a sense of fulfilment. Her journey had come full circle. The lessons she had learned in building and selling her brokerage were now helping a new generation of entrepreneurs.

In the years since selling her business, Sarah had:

1. Founded a successful consulting firm, helping small and medium-sized businesses implement the Four Pillars approach. She had seen companies across various industries transform their operations and achieve remarkable growth.
2. Launched a fintech startup that provided integrated business management software, making data-driven decision-making accessible to businesses of all sizes. The platform had quickly gained traction and was now used by thousands of companies worldwide.

3. Established a non-profit foundation focused on financial literacy education, particularly for young adults and underserved communities. The foundation's programs had reached millions, empowering people to make informed financial decisions.
4. Written a bestselling book, "The Four Pillars of Business Success," which had become required reading in many business schools.
5. Become a respected voice in the business world, frequently sought after for her insights on ethical, sustainable business practices.

But perhaps most gratifyingly, she had seen the lasting impact of her work at her former brokerage. Under DeVere Group's ownership, the business had continued to thrive, expanding its reach while maintaining the core values and practices she had instilled. Many of her former team members had gone on to leadership positions within DeVere Group or had started their own successful ventures, spreading the Four Pillars philosophy even further.

As Sarah stepped down from the podium, her mind drifted to another recent speaking engagement - one that had been simultaneously more nerve-wracking and more rewarding than any business conference.

Just last week, she had been a guest speaker at her children's new school, talking to the students about entrepreneurship and financial literacy. It was a far cry from the days when she had missed school plays and parent-teacher conferences due to work commitments. Now, she had the freedom to be actively involved in her children's education.

Sarah smiled, remembering her children's reactions when they found out she would be speaking at their school. On the surface, they had acted mortified, rolling their eyes and begging her not to embarrass them. But she had caught the proud glances they exchanged when they thought she wasn't looking, and the way they sat up a little straighter in the audience as she spoke.

After her talk, her daughter had approached her, trying to maintain an air of nonchalance. "That wasn't totally cringeworthy, Mum," Lily had said, which Sarah knew was high praise from a teenager. Her son had simply given her a quick hug before darting off to join his friends, but the gesture had spoken volumes.

It was moments like these that made Sarah truly appreciate how far she had come. The success of her business had opened new opportunities, but more importantly, it had given her the freedom to be present for the moments that really mattered.

As Sarah was lost in these thoughts, a young entrepreneur approached her, eyes shining with enthusiasm.

"Ms. Thompson," the young woman said, "your speech was inspiring. I've read your book and have been trying to implement the Four Pillars in my startup. It's challenging, but I'm already seeing results. Thank you for sharing your wisdom."

Sarah smiled warmly, recognising the same passion and determination she had once felt. "The journey isn't always easy," she replied, "but it's incredibly rewarding. Keep pushing forward, stay true to your values, and remember that success is about more than just profits. It's about the lives you touch and the positive change you create."

As she watched the young entrepreneur walk away, filled with new inspiration, Sarah felt a profound sense of gratitude. Her company had been more than just a business; it had been the starting point of a movement towards more ethical, efficient, and impactful business practices.

The Four Pillars - Marketing, Sales, Operations, and Finance - had been the foundation of her success. But it was the integration of these pillars, the way they worked together in harmony, that had truly set her business apart. And now, that integrated approach was helping to shape the future of business.

Sarah left the conference centre and stepped out into the bustling city street. The world of business was ever-changing, presenting new challenges and opportunities. But she knew that the principles she had discovered and refined in her journey would continue to guide entrepreneurs for years to come.

As she hailed a taxi, Sarah's mind was already turning to her next project. There was still so much to do, so many ways to make a positive impact. The summit of success, she had learned, wasn't a final destination. It was a vantage point from which to see new horizons, new mountains to climb.

With a smile on her face and a spring in her step, Sarah set off towards her next adventure. The Four Pillars had taken her further than she had ever imagined, and she couldn't wait to see where they would lead her next.

FINAL CHAPTER SUMMARY: THE SUMMIT OF SUCCESS - YOUR INTEGRATED COMPANY

This final chapter brought together all elements of a successful company, showcasing the power of the Four Pillars approach: Marketing, Sales, Operations, and Finance. Through Sarah's journey, we explored:

1. **The Power of Integration**: How the four pillars work together to create a synergistic, efficient business.
2. **Measurability**: The importance of tracking key metrics across all areas of the business.
3. **Scalability**: How well-designed systems allow for growth without sacrificing quality.
4. **Business Valuation**: How a well-run, measurable business becomes attractive to potential buyers.
5. **Exit Strategy**: The process of considering and ultimately accepting an acquisition offer.
6. **Future Planning**: The importance of personal growth alongside business success.

The chapter emphasised that true success comes not just from excelling in each area, but from creating a harmonious, balanced business that delivers value to clients, satisfaction to the team, and fulfilment to the owner.

Scan here for the WorkBook

FINAL WORKBOOK: IMPLEMENTING THE FOUR PILLARS IN YOUR COMPANY

Part 1: Comprehensive Business Audit

Assess your brokerage across all four pillars. Rate each area from 1 (needs significant improvement) to 10 (excellent):

1. Marketing:

   Key strengths:________________________________

   Areas for improvement: __________________________

2. Sales:

   Key strengths:________________________________

   Areas for improvement: __________________________

3. Operations:

   Key strengths:________________________________

   Areas for improvement: __________________________

4. Finance:

   Key strengths:________________________________

   Areas for improvement: __________________________

Part 2: Integration Plan

Identify three ways each pillar can support the others in your business:

1. How can Marketing support:
    - Sales: ________________
    - Operations: ________________
    - Finance: ________________
2. How can Sales support:
    - Marketing: ________________
    - Operations: ________________
    - Finance: ________________
3. How can Operations support:
    - Marketing: ________________
    - Sales: ________________
    - Finance: ________________
4. How can Finance support:
    - Marketing: ________________
    - Sales: ________________
    - Operations: ________________

Part 3: Key Performance Indicators (KPIs)

List the top 3 KPIs you will track for each pillar:

1. Marketing KPIs:

    a. ________________

    b. ________________

    c. ________________

2. Sales KPIs:
    a. ______________________________
    b. ______________________________
    c. ______________________________
3. Operations KPIs:
    a. ______________________________
    b. ______________________________
    c. ______________________________
4. Finance KPIs:
    a. ______________________________
    b. ______________________________
    c. ______________________________

Part 4: Systematization and Scalability

For each pillar, identify one process you can systemise to improve scalability:

1. Marketing: ______________________________

    Steps to systemise: ______________________________
2. Sales: ______________________________

    Steps to systemise: ______________________________
3. Operations: ______________________________

    Steps to systemise: ______________________________
4. Finance: ______________________________

    Steps to systemise: ______________________________

Part 5: Technology Integration

List one technology solution you can implement for each pillar to improve efficiency:

1. Marketing: ________________________________
2. Sales: ____________________________________
3. Operations: ______________________________
4. Finance: __________________________________

Part 6: Team Development

Identify key roles you need to fill or develop to support each pillar:

1. Marketing: ________________________________
2. Sales: ____________________________________
3. Operations: ______________________________
4. Finance: __________________________________

Part 7: Future Vision

Describe your vision for your company in 3 years:

____

____

____

____

List specific targets for each pillar:

1. Marketing: ________________________________
2. Sales: ____________________________________
3. Operations: ______________________________
4. Finance: __________________________________

Part 8: Personal Development

Identify three skills you need to develop to lead your brokerage to this vision:

1. ______________________________
2. ______________________________
3. ______________________________

Part 9: Exit Strategy Consideration

Even if it's not in your immediate plans, consider your potential exit strategy:

1. What would make your business attractive to potential buyers?

____

____

2. What key metrics would showcase your business's value?

____

____

3. What personal and professional goals would you want to achieve before considering an exit?

____

____

Action Plan

Based on this workbook, list the top 5 actions you will take in the next 90 days to implement the Four Pillars approach in your brokerage:

1. ____
2. ____
3. ____
4. ____
5. ____

Remember, building a successful company is a journey. Regularly revisit this workbook, track your progress, and adjust your strategies as needed. Your goal is to create a balanced, efficient, and valuable business that serves your clients, supports your team, and fulfils your personal and professional aspirations.

"If you don't build your dream, someone else will hire you to help them build theirs."
Dhirubhai Ambani

---

20 REASONS SMALL BUSINESSES FAIL & HOW YOU ARE GOING TO AVOID THEM.

It's a bold move to start your own business & hopefully reading this book as part of your commitment to learning will help you achieve the dreams you started out with.

The idea that being self-employed means you get to start & finish when you want, can take unlimited amounts of holiday and become a legal tax dodger are a million miles from the truth. Reality is, you are now in a world with little support where, if you don't learn to swim very quickly, you'll drown.

So, let's look at some of the disturbing figures before moving on to the top 20 reasons businesses fail and how **YOU** are going to avoid being yet another alarming government statistic.

According to the UK government's business population estimates, the number of new business starts (incorporations) has been fairly consistent in recent years:

- In 2022, approximately 342,000 new businesses were incorporated
- In 2021, around 364,000 new businesses were started
- In 2020, despite the pandemic, there were about 336,000 new business incorporations
- In 2019, before the pandemic, around 382,000 businesses were created

- The years 2018-2022 saw between 336,000 and 382,000 new businesses annually

Taking an average over the past 10 years, the typical number of new businesses started in the UK each year is approximately 350,000. This number can fluctuate based on economic conditions, with notable impacts seen during the COVID-19 pandemic in 2020 and 2021.

It's worth noting that these figures represent incorporated businesses registered with Companies House, which means limited companies. The total number of new businesses, including sole traders and partnerships, might be slightly higher.

These statistics come from the Department for Business and Trade's annual Business Population Estimates, which provide a comprehensive overview of business formation in the United Kingdom.

Business Survival Rates:

- Year 1 Failure Rate: Approximately 20-25% of new businesses fail within their first year
- Year 3 Failure Rate: Around 50-60% of businesses will have ceased trading by their third year
- Year 5 Failure Rate: Roughly 60-70% of businesses will have failed by their fifth year

Factors Contributing to Business Failures:

1. Cash flow problems
2. Lack of market demand
3. Intense competition
4. Poor financial management
5. Insufficient business planning
6. Economic challenges and market conditions

Specific Insights:

- According to the Office for National Statistics (ONS), the five-year survival rate for businesses registered in 2017 was approximately 42.4%
- Small and medium-sized enterprises (SMEs) tend to have higher failure rates compared to larger established businesses
- Certain sectors like technology and professional services have slightly different survival rates compared to traditional industries

The data suggests that while starting a business is challenging, those that survive the first few years have a better chance of long-term success. Proper planning, financial management, and adaptability are crucial for business longevity.

Although these numbers may seem gloomy, the reality is even worse. The key word here is "survival". We're not looking at the number of businesses that are thriving, we're looking at the overall business community and many are just surviving. The biggest indicator to this is highlighted when we look at the actual size of businesses in the UK.

As of 2023, the total number of private sector businesses in the UK is approximately 5.5 million. Here's the detailed breakdown by business size:

- **No Employees (Sole Traders/Freelancers): 4,038,000 (73.4%)**
    - These are typically self-employed individuals, freelancers, and micro-businesses
- **1-10 Employees: 1,124,000 (20.4%)**
    - Small businesses and startups
- **11-20 Employees: 146,000 (2.6%)**
    - Growing small businesses

- **21-50 Employees: 86,000 (1.6%)**
    - Medium-sized businesses
- **51-250 Employees: 44,000 (0.8%)**
    - Larger medium-sized businesses
- **250+ Employees: 8,000 (0.1%)**
    - Large enterprises

Total Registered Businesses: 5,446,000 (100%)

Key Observations:

- **Over 93% of UK businesses have fewer than 10 employees**
- **Large enterprises (250+ employees) make up only 0.1% of businesses**

Source: Department for Business and Trade - Business Population Estimates 2023

So, why is it that so many businesses are started yet nearly half are gone in the first five years and those that "survive" have never really got any further than becoming an unloved employee of their own company. Someone who now likely works for below the minimum hourly rate, with no holiday pay, no sick pay and no employee rights.

Before we move into the TOP 20, lets look at the four stages of learning to perhaps help understand where things are going wrong.

My belief is that many business owners get stuck somewhere between Unconscious Incompetence & Conscious Incompetence but before I insult you any further, let me explain.

From Unconscious Incompetence to Conscious Incompetence

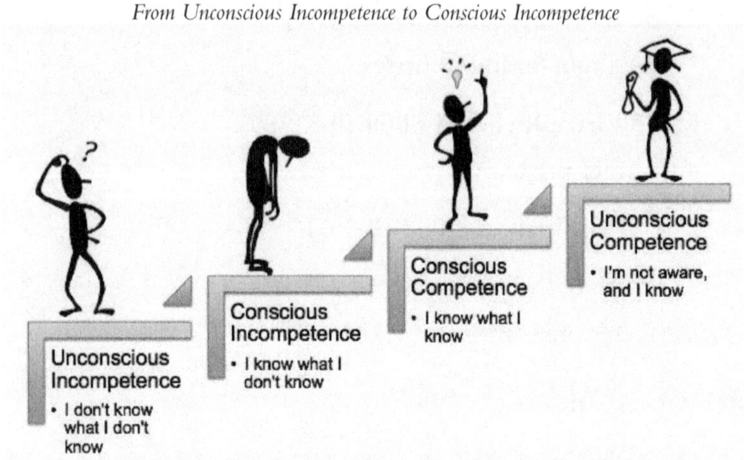

The Four Stages of Learning (Competence Hierarchy):

1. Unconscious Incompetence
   - You don't recognize the skills you lack as a business owner
   - You're unaware of the complexities of running a business
   - You believe it's simpler than it actually is
2. Conscious Incompetence
   - You become aware of how much you don't know about business
   - You recognize the gaps in your knowledge and skills
   - You understand the challenges of entrepreneurship
3. Conscious Competence
   - You've learned business skills but must think carefully about each decision
   - You can manage your business, but it requires constant concentration
   - Each strategic move is deliberate and requires focus

4. Unconscious Competence
    - Business management becomes intuitive
    - You make complex decisions almost automatically
    - Your experience guides you effortlessly through challenges

Using The Driving Analogy for Business Ownership:

Stage 1 (Unconscious Incompetence): Imagine you're a teenager who thinks driving is easy. You've watched people drive and believe, "How hard can this be? I'll just sit down, turn the key, and go!" You have no idea about checking mirrors, understanding road rules, managing speed, or handling unexpected situations. In business, this is like thinking you can run a company simply because you have a good idea.

Stage 2 (Conscious Incompetence): Your first driving lesson arrives. Suddenly, you realize driving is complicated. You're stalling the car, struggling to coordinate clutch and accelerator, checking mirrors feels overwhelming, and navigating traffic seems impossible. This mirrors the moment in business when you realize running a company is far more complex than you imagined. You start to understand the vast amount you need to learn about marketing, sales & finance. You're now starting to lose confidence in your ability to deliver in the operations box, which is the very reason you started your business.

Stage 3 (Conscious Competence): Now you're driving, but it takes all your concentration. You're checking mirrors meticulously, thinking about every gear change, carefully watching speed limits, and planning your route. Your hands are gripping the steering wheel tightly. In business, this is when you're consciously applying learned skills. Every business decision requires careful thought. You're following guidelines, double-checking financials, carefully planning marketing strategies, and managing every detail with intense focus.

Stage 4 (Unconscious Competence): Eventually, driving becomes second nature. You can navigate complex routes, handle unexpected traffic, adjust to different road conditions, and have conversations while driving without thinking about the mechanics. Similarly, in business, you reach a point where strategic decisions flow naturally. You intuitively understand market dynamics, make quick decisions, manage teams effortlessly, and navigate business challenges with ease.

The Journey of Learning: Just like learning to drive, becoming a successful business owner is a progressive journey. You start with zero knowledge, gradually gain skills through practice and learning, and eventually develop an intuitive understanding that makes complex tasks seem simple.

Key Insights:

- Everyone starts as a beginner
- Learning is a continuous process
- Patience and persistent learning are crucial
- Mistakes are part of the learning journey
- Each stage builds the foundation for the next

The most successful business owners are those who:

- Recognise their limitations
- Are eager to learn
- Stay humble
- Adapt continuously
- View challenges as opportunities for growth

Remember, no one becomes an expert overnight. Whether driving or running a business, mastery comes from consistent effort, learning from mistakes, and a willingness to improve step by step. And this is where I think many businesses fail.

Whether you are a great plumber, the most creative florist or the most knowledgeable mortgage broker, these skills just get you a job, they don't get you a business. As you've discovered through this book, you need to have all four pillars covered to create something that's going to support you & your family, without killing you in the process. My belief is, many of the business owners that fail or only survive never get beyond Unconscious Incompetence. They simply don't know what they do know. Those that do get to the next stage of Conscious Incompetence are simply overwhelmed and don't know what the next steps are, they just know that they don't know.

Our aim at Grow Partnership, & one of the key reasons for writing this book is to help **1 million business owners** realise that business can be fun, engaging and fulfilling. If you are a sole trader and wish to stay that way through lifestyle choice, then that's absolutely fine. If you are in the 1 to 10 employee group and living the dream, then good luck, you're so much further than most. But if you're struggling & life is miserable then, as Jim Rohn so eloquently puts it.....

"Don't wish it were easier; wish you were better. Don't wish for less problems, wish for more skills. Don't wish for less challenge, wish for more wisdom. Work harder on yourself than you do on your job."

THE TOP 20 REASONS BUSINESSES FAIL

And what you are now going to do to prevent it happening to you.

The top 20 business failure points comes with a list of actions you can take to avoid each stage. Please don't be overwhelmed by the list, thinking you have too much to take on. Simply use each list as a check sheet to work on. If it helps you focus and you start working through one process at a time, you'll not only build a sustainable business, but it'll be in a shape that you can step back from whilst still achieving a great income.

If you're impatient and looking to take instant action, before you get to the full list of 20, I've listed what I feel are the five key areas to focus on in any business and some simple steps to get you going forward.

1. **IMPLEMENT A ROBUST SYSTEMS AND MEASUREMENT APPROACH**

Document all key processes as SOPs: Start by listing everything you do in a week. Take the top three most frequent activities and write down step-by-step how you complete these tasks. Be specific - include which buttons to click, what to say, what to check. Test these instructions by having someone else follow them. Refine based on their feedback. Once you have these three documented successfully, move onto the next three most frequent activities. Within a month, you'll have your core business documented.

Create clear KPIs for each business area: Choose just three numbers that would tell you if your business is healthy - perhaps number of new enquiries, conversion rate, and average case value. Create a simple spreadsheet and start tracking these daily or weekly. Once this becomes habit, add three more measures. Keep it simple - a complex reporting system you don't use is worse than a simple one you do.

Implement proper technology solutions: Don't try to implement everything at once. Start with a CRM system - it's the foundation of most business automation. Spend time researching the right one for your business, then implement it fully before moving to other technology. Better to have one system working well than several working poorly.

Regular performance monitoring: Set aside 30 minutes every Monday morning to review your key numbers from the previous week. Make this unmissable - like a client appointment. Use this time to spot trends and make one adjustment to improve performance. Just one change per week - consistency beats intensity.

Clear reporting structures: Create a simple one-page dashboard showing your key metrics. Update it weekly. Share relevant parts with your team. Make it visual - graphs are better than numbers for spotting trends. Keep it simple enough that anyone could understand it at a glance.

2. CREATE A CLIENT-FOCUSED STRATEGY

Define your ideal client profile: Look at your last 20 clients. Identify the five you most enjoyed working with and were most profitable. List everything they have in common - not just basic demographics, but their attitudes, values, and behaviours. This is your ideal client profile. Write it down in detail. Now look at what these clients needed from you and ensure your service perfectly matches these needs. This becomes your target market focus.

Develop clear value proposition: Write down every step of your service delivery and the specific value each step brings to your ideal client. Focus on outcomes, not features. For example, don't say "we offer mortgage advice" but rather "we help first-time buyers navigate the complex mortgage process, ensuring they get the best deal for their circumstances while avoiding common costly mistakes." Test this message with existing clients to refine it.

Create systematic follow-up processes: Build a simple follow-up calendar. Start with just three touchpoints: immediate response to enquiry, 48-hour check-in, and one-week follow-up. Script these interactions and save them as templates. Once this becomes routine, add more touchpoints. Use your CRM to automate these where possible, but always personalise the message. Remember, automation should enhance the personal touch, not replace it.

Build strong client relationships: Create a simple client information sheet capturing not just basic details but personal information - children's names, hobbies, important dates. Review this before every client interaction. Set up Google alerts for their business or industry. Make notes after every interaction about what you discussed personally, not just business matters. This helps make future conversations more meaningful.

Regular client feedback and review systems: Start with a simple three-question survey after each transaction: What did we do well? What could we improve? Would you recommend us? Make it easy to respond - email, text, or online form. Actually use the feedback - review it monthly and make one improvement based on what you learn. Share improvements with clients who suggested them - they'll appreciate being heard.

3. ESTABLISH A STRONG TEAM DEVELOPMENT PROGRAMME

Proper recruitment using a character profiling tool such as DISC: Before hiring anyone, write down exactly what personality type would best suit the role. Use DISC profiling during recruitment - many online providers offer this service cost-effectively. Don't just hire people like yourself. If you're great with clients but poor with details, hire someone detail-oriented. Create a balanced team with complementary strengths.

Comprehensive training systems: Start with a basic checklist of everything a new team member needs to know in their first week, month, and three months. Break these down into daily training sessions of no more than 30 minutes. Create short video recordings of yourself performing key tasks - these become training resources. Have new team members create their own notes during training - these often become your best process documents.

Clear roles and responsibilities: Create a simple one-page document for each role listing their key responsibilities, success measures, and authority levels. Be specific about what decisions they can make without consultation. Review this document with each team member monthly - it will evolve as they grow in capability. It's important that each team member knows what a "great day" looks like for them. This helps them take responsibility and grow into the role.

Regular performance reviews: Schedule monthly 30-minute check-ins with each team member. Use the same format each time: What's going well? Where do you need support? What are your goals for next month? What do you need from me? Keep notes and review progress each month. This consistency builds trust and improves performance.

Effective delegation processes: Start small - identify three tasks you currently do that could be delegated. Document these clearly. Train someone to do them. Check their work initially, then gradually reduce oversight as they prove capability. Once these are successfully delegated, identify three more tasks. Within months you'll have freed up significant time for strategic work.

4. DEVELOP A KNOWLEDGE AND GROWTH MINDSET

Regular professional development: Block out two hours every week for learning - treat it like an important client meeting. Use this time to read industry publications, take online courses, or watch educational videos. Create a simple learning log: What did I learn? How can I apply this? Who else needs to know this? Share relevant insights with your team in a weekly email or meeting. This creates a culture of continuous learning.

Strategic networking: Identify the top five professionals who regularly work with your ideal clients (e.g., estate agents, accountants, solicitors for a Mortgage Broker). Meet each one for coffee monthly. Don't sell - focus on understanding their business challenges and finding ways to help them. Create a simple introducer pack showing how you can add value to their clients. Follow up every introduction promptly and keep them informed of outcomes.

Expert advisor relationships: Start with one key advisor - perhaps an accountant or business coach. Meet quarterly to review your business performance and plans. Be completely honest about challenges - they can't help if they don't know the real situation. Implement their advice and show them the results. Once this relationship is working well, add another advisor with different expertise.

Innovation monitoring: Subscribe to three industry newsletters and spend 15 minutes each morning reviewing them. Set up Google alerts for key industry terms. Join relevant LinkedIn groups. Create a simple system to capture ideas - perhaps a notes app on your phone. Review these ideas monthly and choose one to implement. Start small - test new ideas with a few trusted clients before rolling out widely.

Industry engagement: Join your main industry association and attend at least one event quarterly. Volunteer to speak or contribute articles - this positions you as an expert. Create content from your daily client interactions - common questions become blog posts or social media content. Share your expertise freely - it returns value many times over.

5. IMPLEMENT ROBUST FINANCIAL CONTROLS

Clear financial reporting: Create a simple one-page financial dashboard showing key numbers: revenue, costs, profit, cash position. Update this weekly - it takes 10 minutes once set up. Review it every Monday morning. Look for trends, not just numbers. When something looks wrong, investigate immediately. Small issues are easy to fix; big ones often start as small ones ignored.

Regular cash flow monitoring: Create a rolling 13-week cash flow forecast. Update it every Monday. Record every expected inflow and outflow. Be conservative with income predictions and generous with expense estimates. Maintain a cash buffer of at least two months' operating costs. Review aged debtors weekly and chase promptly - late payments often become bad debts.

Proper pricing strategies: Calculate your true hourly cost by including ALL expenses and desired profit. Work out how many billable hours you really have (hint: it's usually less than you think). Use this to set minimum pricing levels. Review pricing quarterly. Don't compete on price - compete on value. Raise prices regularly in small increments rather than large jumps occasionally.

Multiple revenue streams: List all your current services. Identify three ways to create recurring revenue - perhaps review services or retainer arrangements. Start with your best clients - offer them enhanced service packages. Create strategic partnerships to earn referral income. Test new services with existing clients before marketing widely.

Regular financial review process: Schedule monthly financial reviews - look at actual versus planned performance. Investigate variances. Look for opportunities to reduce costs without sacrificing quality. Review supplier contracts annually.

Keep your accountant informed of plans - they often spot potential issues before they become problems. Act quickly on negative trends - hope is not a strategy.

Remember, implementation is about progress, not perfection. Start with the areas that will make the biggest difference to your business and build from there. Regular small improvements compound into significant changes over time.

So, on to the list.....

1. INADEQUATE PLANNING & MARKET RESEARCH

Sarah's Story: Like many business owners, Sarah initially launched her mortgage brokerage with enthusiasm but without a clear plan. She was confident in her ability to arrange mortgages but hadn't thoroughly researched her market or developed a structured business plan.

The Failure Point: Many small businesses fail before they truly begin because of inadequate planning and market research. Entrepreneurs often rush into business based on their technical skills or passion for their industry, without understanding their target market, competition, or unique selling proposition. They fail to consider crucial elements like startup costs, operating expenses, and realistic revenue projections.

This lack of planning frequently leads to cash flow problems within the first year. Without understanding their market, businesses struggle to differentiate themselves from competitors and often end up competing solely on price, leading to unsustainable profit margins.

Additionally, inadequate planning means businesses aren't prepared for seasonal fluctuations, market changes, or unexpected challenges. They react to situations rather than anticipating and preparing for them, putting them at a significant disadvantage.

How You Are Going to Avoid This Point:

1. Develop a comprehensive business plan that includes:
    - Detailed market analysis
    - Competitor research
    - Clear financial projections
    - Marketing strategy
    - Operational requirements
2. Conduct thorough market research:
    - Survey potential customers
    - Analyse competitor offerings
    - Identify market gaps and opportunities
    - Understand industry trends
3. Create contingency plans:
    - Build emergency funds
    - Identify potential risks
    - Develop mitigation strategies
    - Plan for seasonal variations
4. Set measurable goals:
    - Short-term (90 days)
    - Medium-term (1 year)
    - Long-term (3-5 years)
    - Regular review and adjustment of these goals

2. POOR FINANCIAL MANAGEMENT

Sarah's Story: In the early days, Sarah managed her business finances by simply checking her bank balance. She had no clear understanding of her profit margins, cash flow cycles, or true operating costs. Her wake-up call came when she faced a cash flow crisis despite having a seemingly healthy business.

The Failure Point: Poor financial management is one of the most lethal business killers. Many small business owners confuse revenue with profit and cash flow with success. They fail to understand their true operating costs, don't maintain adequate cash reserves, and have no system for monitoring key financial metrics.

This lack of financial acumen often leads to pricing errors, unsustainable overhead costs, and dangerous cash flow gaps. Businesses might appear profitable on paper but still fail due to poor cash flow management or unexpected expenses. Many owners don't realise they're in trouble until it's too late to correct course.

How You Are Going to Avoid This Point:

1. Implement robust financial tracking:
    - Set up proper accounting systems
    - Monitor key financial metrics daily/weekly
    - Create regular financial reports
    - Understand your key numbers
2. Maintain cash reserves:
    - Build a minimum three-month operating cost buffer
    - Plan for seasonal variations
    - Establish clear credit control procedures
    - Create emergency contingency plans
3. Get professional help:
    - Hire a qualified accountant
    - Regular financial reviews
    - Professional bookkeeping support
    - Financial forecasting assistance
4. Monitor key metrics:
    - Track profit margins by service/product

- Monitor cash flow weekly
- Review overhead costs monthly
- Analyse revenue trends

3. LACK OF SYSTEMS AND PROCESSES

Sarah's Story: Initially, Sarah ran her business on memory and intuition. Every task required her involvement, and there was no standardisation in how things were done. This not only led to inconsistent service quality but also made it impossible for her to scale the business or take time off.

The Failure Point: Many businesses operate in a constant state of chaos because they lack proper systems and processes. Every task becomes an exercise in reinventing the wheel, leading to wasted time, inconsistent quality, and increased stress. Without documented procedures, businesses can't effectively train new staff, maintain quality standards, or operate efficiently.

This systemic failure often results in:

- Missed opportunities due to poor organisation
- Increased costs from repeated mistakes
- Higher staff turnover due to frustration
- Inability to scale the business
- Complete dependence on the owner

How You Are Going to Avoid This Point:

1. Document core processes:
    - Create detailed Standard Operating Procedures (SOPs)
    - Build process flowcharts
    - Develop quality control checklists
    - Establish clear workflows

2. Implement technology solutions:
   - Choose appropriate CRM systems
   - Automate repetitive tasks
   - Use project management tools
   - Integrate key business applications
3. Create training systems:
   - Develop onboarding procedures
   - Build training manuals
   - Create video tutorials
   - Establish mentoring programmes
4. Regular review and refinement:
   - Monitor system effectiveness
   - Gather team feedback
   - Update procedures as needed
   - Measure efficiency improvements

4. INSUFFICIENT CASH FLOW MANAGEMENT

Sarah's Story: Like many brokers, Sarah initially struggled with the feast-and-famine cycle of commission income. She would have months of strong earnings followed by periods of minimal income, yet her business expenses remained constant. Through Michelle's guidance, she learned to forecast and manage her cash flow effectively.

The Failure Point: Cash flow problems kill otherwise viable businesses every day. Many business owners fail to understand that profit doesn't equal cash flow. A business can be profitable on paper but still fail due to poor cash flow management. This is particularly true in service-based businesses where income can be irregular or seasonal.

The impact of poor cash flow management often manifests as:

- Inability to meet regular financial commitments
- Stressed relationships with suppliers
- Missed opportunities due to lack of available funds
- Personal financial strain on the owner
- Difficulty in planning for growth or investment

How You Are Going to Avoid This Point:

1. Implement cash flow forecasting:
    - Create rolling 12-month cash flow forecasts
    - Monitor cash flow weekly
    - Plan for seasonal variations
    - Build cash reserves during strong periods
2. Manage receivables effectively:
    - Clear payment terms
    - Prompt invoicing
    - Regular follow-up on overdue payments
    - Consider factoring or invoice financing options
3. Control expenses:
    - Regular review of all costs
    - Negotiate better supplier terms
    - Monitor subscriptions and recurring charges
    - Build emergency reserves
4. Diversify income streams:
    - Develop multiple revenue sources
    - Create recurring revenue models where possible
    - Build strategic partnerships
    - Consider complementary services

5. NO CLEAR TARGET MARKET OR POSITIONING

Sarah's Story: When Sarah first started her brokerage, she tried to be everything to everyone. She took on any client who came her way, regardless of whether their needs aligned with her strengths. This scattered approach led to inefficiencies, stress, and inconsistent results until Michelle helped her define her ideal client profile.

The Failure Point: Many businesses fail because they lack focus in their target market and positioning. Trying to serve everyone typically results in serving no one particularly well. This unfocused approach leads to:

- Ineffective marketing efforts
- Higher customer acquisition costs
- Difficulty in building expertise and reputation
- Inconsistent service delivery
- Lower profit margins due to constant adaptation

Without a clear target market, businesses struggle to develop effective marketing messages, build relevant expertise, or create efficient systems. They often end up competing solely on price, leading to unsustainable business models.

How You Are Going to Avoid This Point:

1. Define your ideal client:
    - Create detailed client avatars
    - Identify their specific needs and pain points
    - Understand their decision-making process
    - Document where to find them
2. Analyse your strengths:
    - Identify your unique capabilities
    - Define your best areas of expertise

    - Review your most successful past clients
    - Understand what you do better than competitors

3. Position your business:
    - Develop a clear unique value proposition
    - Create targeted marketing messages
    - Build relevant case studies
    - Focus your service offerings
4. Regular review and refinement:
    - Track client satisfaction by segment
    - Monitor profitability by client type
    - Adjust targeting based on results
    - Stay focused on your chosen market

6. INADEQUATE SALES PROCESS AND FOLLOW-UP

Sarah's Story: Initially, Sarah's sales process was entirely reactive and inconsistent. Each client interaction was different, and she had no system for following up with prospects who weren't immediately ready to proceed.Through Michelle's guidance, she developed a structured, consultative approach that dramatically improved her conversion rates.

The Failure Point: Many businesses fail due to poorly structured sales processes and inconsistent follow-up. Without a systematic approach to sales, businesses:

- Miss opportunities with potential clients
- Waste time on unqualified prospects
- Deliver inconsistent client experiences
- Struggle to train new team members
- Fail to build long-term relationships

This lack of process often results in feast-or-famine cycles, where businesses frantically chase new clients rather than nurturing existing relationships and leads.

How You Are Going to Avoid This Point:

1. Develop a structured sales process:
    - Create clear stages for client engagement
    - Build consultation frameworks
    - Develop standard questions and responses
    - Implement quality control checkpoints
2. Create a follow-up system:
    - Implement a CRM system
    - Develop automated follow-up sequences
    - Create reminder systems
    - Track all client interactions
3. Build relationship management processes:
    - Regular client review schedules
    - Systematic communication plans
    - Referral request systems
    - Client satisfaction surveys
4. Measure and improve:
    - Track conversion rates
    - Monitor client acquisition costs
    - Analyse lost opportunities
    - Regularly review and refine processes

7. POOR TEAM DEVELOPMENT AND MANAGEMENT

Sarah's Story: When Sarah first started hiring, she chose people similar to herself, leading to gaps in team capabilities. Michelle introduced her to DISC profiling and proper recruitment processes, helping her build a balanced team with complementary strengths.

The Failure Point: Many businesses fail because they can't build and retain effective teams. Common issues include:

- Poor hiring decisions based on gut feel rather than structured assessment
- Lack of proper training and development programmes
- Unclear expectations and role definitions
- Ineffective delegation due to trust issues
- High staff turnover from poor management
- Micromanagement stifling team growth and innovation

This failure in team development creates a constant cycle of recruitment, training, and replacement that drains resources and prevents business growth. Moreover, poor team management often leads to decreased morale, reduced productivity, and missed business opportunities.

How You Are Going to Avoid This Point:

1. Implement proper recruitment processes:
    - Use personality profiling tools like DISC
    - Create detailed job descriptions with clear expectations
    - Develop structured interview processes
    - Check references thoroughly
    - Test for cultural fit as well as skills
2. Establish comprehensive training systems:
    - Create detailed onboarding programmes

- Develop ongoing training schedules
- Build clear career progression paths
- Implement mentoring systems
- Regular skill development workshops

3. Set clear expectations:
    - Define specific roles and responsibilities
    - Establish measurable performance metrics
    - Create accountability systems
    - Conduct regular performance reviews
    - Clear communication channels
4. Foster team development:
    - Regular team meetings and updates
    - Professional development opportunities
    - Recognition and reward programmes
    - Team building activities
    - Create a positive work culture

8. RESISTANCE TO TECHNOLOGY AND CHANGE

Sarah's Story: Sarah initially resisted adopting new technology, fearing it would make her service impersonal. Through Michelle's guidance, she learned that technology could enhance her personal service by freeing up time for meaningful client interactions.

The Failure Point: Many businesses fail because they refuse to adapt to changing technology and market conditions. This resistance often stems from:

- Fear of change
- Comfort with familiar methods
- Concerns about implementation costs

- Worry about disrupting existing processes
- Lack of understanding of potential benefits

This resistance leaves businesses struggling with inefficient manual processes while competitors gain advantages through automation and innovation.

How You Are Going to Avoid This Point:

1. Assess current technology needs:
    - Audit existing systems
    - Identify process bottlenecks
    - Research available solutions
    - Calculate potential ROI
2. Plan strategic implementation:
    - Start with critical systems
    - Train staff properly
    - Monitor effectiveness
    - Gather user feedback
3. Stay informed about innovations:
    - Join industry groups
    - Attend technology seminars
    - Network with peers
    - Regular market research
4. Measure impact:
    - Track efficiency improvements
    - Monitor cost savings
    - Assess customer satisfaction
    - Review staff productivity

9. INCONSISTENT SERVICE DELIVERY

Sarah's Story: Early in her business journey, Sarah's service quality varied depending on her workload and stress levels. Some clients received exceptional service while others experienced delays and communication gaps. Through implementing proper systems and quality control measures, she ensured every client received consistently high service levels regardless of circumstances.

The Failure Point: Many businesses struggle to maintain consistent service quality as they grow. This inconsistency stems from:

- Lack of standardised procedures
- Over-reliance on individual staff members
- Poor quality control measures
- Inadequate training and support
- Reactive rather than proactive service delivery

This inconsistency leads to:

- Damaged reputation
- Lost repeat business
- Reduced referrals
- Higher customer acquisition costs
- Increased staff stress and turnover

How You Are Going to Avoid This Point:

1. Establish service standards:
    - Create detailed service level agreements
    - Define key quality metrics
    - Set clear response time expectations
    - Develop customer journey maps
    - Regular quality audits

2. Implement quality control measures:
   - Regular service reviews
   - Client feedback systems
   - Mystery shopping programmes
   - Performance monitoring
   - Regular team training
3. Build support systems:
   - Clear escalation procedures
   - Back-up staff arrangements
   - Emergency response plans
   - Resource allocation systems
   - Regular capacity reviews
4. Monitor and improve:
   - Track customer satisfaction scores
   - Analyse complaint patterns
   - Regular service audits
   - Team feedback sessions
   - Continuous improvement programmes

10. POOR WORK-LIFE BALANCE AND BURNOUT

Sarah's Story: Initially, Sarah was working endless hours, missing family events, and heading towards burnout. Through Michelle's guidance, she learned that sustainable business success required a balanced approach to work and life, implementing systems that allowed the business to thrive without consuming her entire life.

The Failure Point: Many business owners fail due to physical and emotional exhaustion. This burnout often results from:

- Excessive working hours

- Inability to switch off
- Constant stress and pressure
- Neglected personal relationships
- Poor health management
- No time for strategic thinking

The impact extends beyond personal wellbeing to affect:

- Decision-making ability
- Team morale
- Service quality
- Business growth potential
- Long-term sustainability

How You Are Going to Avoid This Point:

1. Create boundaries:
    - Set clear working hours
    - Establish 'no-work' zones
    - Schedule family time
    - Plan regular breaks
    - Learn to say 'no'
2. Implement delegation systems:
    - Train team members effectively
    - Clear authority levels
    - Document procedures
    - Trust-building exercises
    - Regular team reviews
3. Focus on efficiency:
    - Prioritise important tasks
    - Eliminate timewasters

    - Use technology effectively
    - Streamline processes
    - Regular workflow reviews

4. Maintain personal wellbeing:
    - Regular exercise
    - Proper nutrition
    - Adequate sleep
    - Stress management techniques
    - Regular health check-ups

11. INEFFECTIVE MARKETING STRATEGY

Sarah's Story: Initially, Sarah relied solely on random referrals and occasional social media posts. Through Michelle's guidance, she developed a comprehensive marketing strategy that consistently attracted her ideal clients and measured the return on every marketing investment.

The Failure Point: Many businesses fail because they lack a coherent marketing strategy. Common issues include:

- Random, unplanned marketing activities
- No clear message or positioning
- Inability to measure marketing effectiveness
- Inconsistent brand presence
- Poor understanding of target audience needs

This lack of strategic marketing leads to:

- Wasted marketing spend
- Inconsistent lead flow
- Higher client acquisition costs
- Missed opportunities
- Poor market positioning

How You Are Going to Avoid This Point:

1. Develop a clear marketing plan:
    - Define target audience
    - Create clear messaging
    - Set measurable goals
    - Establish marketing budget
    - Choose appropriate channels
2. Implement measurement systems:
    - Track all marketing activities
    - Monitor return on investment
    - Analyse lead sources
    - Review conversion rates
    - Regular performance reviews
3. Build brand consistency:
    - Create brand guidelines
    - Develop content strategy
    - Plan regular communications
    - Maintain professional image
    - Monitor brand perception
4. Regular review and adjustment:
    - Monthly performance analysis
    - Quarterly strategy reviews
    - Test new approaches
    - Refine successful activities
    - Abandon ineffective tactics

12. POOR PRICING STRATEGY

Sarah's Story: Like many business owners, Sarah initially set her prices by matching competitors and hoping for the best. Like many business owners, Sarah's strategy of offering more than her competitors but at a lower rate than they were charging just leads to "a race to the bottom" and burn-out through trying to make a profit whilst not charging the right rate to the right client. Michelle helped her understand her true value and costs, leading to a pricing structure that reflected her expertise while ensuring profitability.

The Failure Point: Businesses often fail due to ineffective pricing strategies. Common issues include:

- Undervaluing services/products
- Not understanding true costs
- Price-based competition
- Lack of value communication
- Fear of charging premium rates

The impact extends to:

- Unsustainable profit margins
- Inability to invest in growth
- Poor quality service delivery
- Staff retention issues
- Reduced business value

How You Are Going to Avoid This Point:

1. Understand your costs:
    - Calculate all direct costs
    - Account for overhead
    - Factor in development time
    - Include profit margins

- Regular cost reviews

2. Value-based pricing:
   - Identify unique value proposition
   - Research market positioning
   - Understand client perception
   - Document results achieved
   - Track client outcomes
3. Develop pricing strategy:
   - Create clear pricing tiers
   - Set minimum profitability levels
   - Regular market analysis
   - Monitor competitor positioning
   - Review pricing quarterly
4. Communicate value effectively:
   - Clear value proposition
   - Case study development
   - Client testimonials
   - ROI demonstrations
   - Regular client education

13. INADEQUATE CLIENT RELATIONSHIP MANAGEMENT

Sarah's Story: Early in her business, Sarah focused solely on acquiring new clients whilst neglecting existing relationships. Through implementing a Client Satisfaction Manager role and systematic review process, she transformed one-off transactions into lasting, profitable relationships.

- **The Failure Point:** Many businesses fail because they don't maintain strong client relationships. Key issues include:

- No systematic follow-up
- Poor communication
- Missed renewal opportunities
- Lost referral opportunities
- Lack of client feedback systems

This neglect leads to:

- Higher client acquisition costs
- Reduced lifetime value
- Lower referral rates
- Damaged reputation
- Inconsistent revenue

How You Are Going to Avoid This Point:

1. Implement CRM system:
    - Regular client contact schedule
    - Automated follow-up systems
    - Client history tracking
    - Communication logs
    - Relationship milestones
2. Develop review process:
    - Regular client reviews
    - Satisfaction surveys
    - Feedback mechanisms
    - Issue resolution procedures
    - Service improvement tracking
3. Create value-add programmes:
    - Client education initiatives
    - Regular market updates

- Special client events
- Loyalty rewards
- Referral incentives

1. Monitor relationship health:

- Track client satisfaction
- Measure retention rates
- Monitor referral rates
- Review feedback trends
- Regular relationship audits

14. RESISTANCE TO PROFESSIONAL ADVICE

Sarah's Story: Initially, Sarah tried to handle everything herself, resisting professional guidance. Working with Michelle taught her the value of expert advice in accelerating business growth and avoiding costly mistakes.

The Failure Point: Many business owners fail because they:

- Avoid seeking professional help
- Try to be experts in everything
- Make preventable mistakes
- Miss growth opportunities
- Waste time reinventing solutions

This resistance often stems from:

- Cost concerns
- Control issues
- Pride
- Lack of trust
- Short-term thinking

How You Are Going to Avoid This Point:

1. Build a professional network:
   - Identify key advisors needed
   - Research qualifications
   - Check references
   - Regular review meetings
   - Clear communication channels
2. Maximise advisor value:
   - Prepare for meetings
   - Implement recommendations
   - Track results
   - Regular reviews
   - Share business goals
3. Budget for expertise:
   - Allocate advisory budget
   - Track ROI on advice
   - Plan strategic investments
   - Regular cost reviews
   - Value assessment
4. Create advisory board:
   - Select complementary expertise
   - Regular meetings
   - Clear objectives
   - Implementation plans
   - Performance tracking

15. POOR RISK MANAGEMENT

Sarah's Story: Initially operating without contingency plans, Sarah learned through Michelle's guidance to identify and prepare for potential risks, from staff illness to market downturns.

The Failure Point: Businesses often fail due to inadequate risk management:

- No contingency planning
- Insufficient insurance
- Poor compliance management
- Over-reliance on key individuals
- Inadequate documentation

This leads to:

- Unexpected crises
- Business interruptions
- Legal issues
- Financial losses
- Reputational damage

How You Are Going to Avoid This Point:

1. Identify potential risks:
    - Regular risk assessments
    - Market analysis
    - Compliance reviews
    - Staff dependencies
    - System vulnerabilities
2. Develop mitigation strategies:
    - Contingency plans
    - Insurance coverage

- Back-up systems
- Staff cross-training
- Emergency procedures

3. Regular review and updates:
   - Monthly risk reviews
   - Update procedures
   - Test emergency plans
   - Staff training
   - Documentation updates
4. Create risk management culture:
   - Staff awareness training
   - Regular updates
   - Clear procedures
   - Reporting systems
   - Review processes

16. INSUFFICIENT BUSINESS DOCUMENTATION

Sarah's Story: Early in her business, Sarah kept everything in her head. Michelle helped her understand the importance of proper documentation for both operational efficiency and business value.

The Failure Point: Many businesses fail due to poor documentation:

- No written procedures
- Informal agreements
- Poor record keeping
- Unclear policies
- Missing compliance records

Impact includes:

- Operational inefficiencies
- Legal vulnerabilities
- Training difficulties
- Reduced business value
- Compliance risks

How You Are Going to Avoid This Point:

1. Create documentation system:
    - Standard operating procedures
    - Policy manuals
    - Process flowcharts
    - Training materials
    - Compliance records
2. Implement document management:
    - Central storage system
    - Access controls
    - Version control
    - Regular updates
    - Back-up procedures
3. Maintain records:
    - Client interactions
    - Financial transactions
    - Staff matters
    - Legal agreements
    - Compliance activities
4. Regular reviews:
    - Update procedures

    - Audit documentation
    - Check compliance
    - Staff training
    - System improvements

17. POOR NETWORKING AND RELATIONSHIP BUILDING

Sarah's Story: Initially focused solely on direct client work, Sarah learned the value of building strategic relationships with introducers and industry partners.

The Failure Point: Businesses often fail due to isolation:

- Limited professional network
- Few strategic partnerships
- Poor industry connections
- Missed opportunities
- Limited market influence

Impact includes:

- Reduced referral sources
- Limited growth opportunities
- Slower problem solving
- Missed market insights
- Reduced business value

How You Are Going to Avoid This Point:

1. Build strategic relationships:
    - Identify key partners
    - Regular networking
    - Industry involvement
    - Professional associations

    - Community engagement

2. Maintain relationships:
    - Regular contact
    - Value exchange
    - Joint initiatives
    - Referral tracking
    - Partnership reviews
3. Create networking strategy:
    - Target event selection
    - Clear objectives
    - Follow-up system
    - Value proposition
    - Results tracking
4. Leverage relationships:
    - Joint marketing
    - Knowledge sharing
    - Resource pooling
    - Cross-referrals
    - Strategic alliances

18. POOR SUCCESSION PLANNING

Sarah's Story: Through Michelle's guidance, Sarah learned to build her business with eventual succession in mind, creating systems and processes that would work without her.

The Failure Point: Many businesses fail due to poor succession planning:

- Owner dependence
- No exit strategy
- Undocumented processes

- Poor delegation
- Limited scalability

Impact includes:

- Reduced business value
- Limited growth potential
- Staff uncertainty
- Missed opportunities
- Business vulnerability

How You Are Going to Avoid This Point:

1. Create succession plan:
    - Identify key roles
    - Document processes
    - Train successors
    - Transfer relationships
    - Timeline development
2. Build business value:
    - Systemise operations
    - Document procedures
    - Develop team
    - Create assets
    - Measure performance
3. Prepare for transition:
    - Legal preparation
    - Financial planning
    - Staff communication
    - Client management
    - Timeline execution

4. Regular review:
    - Plan updates
    - Progress monitoring
    - Team development
    - Value assessment
    - Strategy adjustment

19. INSUFFICIENT INNOVATION

Sarah's Story: Initially stuck in traditional methods, Sarah learned to embrace innovation in service delivery, client communication, and business operations.

The Failure Point: Businesses fail through lack of innovation:

- Outdated methods
- Resistance to change
    - Market irrelevance
    - Competitor vulnerability
    - Missed opportunities

Impact includes:

- Reduced competitiveness
- Lower efficiency
- Higher costs
- Market share loss
- Reduced profitability

How You Are Going to Avoid This Point:

1. Foster innovation culture:
    - Encourage ideas
    - Test new approaches

    - Learn from failures
    - Reward creativity
    - Regular reviews

2. Monitor trends:
    - Industry developments
    - Technology changes
    - Client needs
    - Competitor analysis
    - Market shifts

3. Implement changes:
    - Pilot testing
    - Measured rollout
    - Staff training
    - Client communication
    - Performance monitoring

4. Regular review:
    - Results analysis
    - Strategy adjustment
    - Team feedback
    - Client feedback
    - Market response

20. POOR PERSONAL DEVELOPMENT

Sarah's Story: Through working with Michelle, Sarah learned the importance of continuous personal development alongside business growth.

The Failure Point: Business owners often fail due to:

- Stagnant skills

- Limited perspective
- Poor leadership
- Outdated knowledge
- Resistance to learning

Impact includes:

- Limited business growth
- Poor decision making
- Team dissatisfaction
- Missed opportunities
- Reduced business value

How You Are Going to Avoid This Point:

1. Create development plan:
    - Skill assessment
    - Learning objectives
    - Training schedule
    - Mentorship opportunities
    - Progress tracking
2. Implement learning:
    - Regular training
    - Industry education
    - Leadership development
    - Peer learning
    - Professional coaching
3. Monitor progress:
    - Skills assessment
    - Knowledge application
    - Results measurement

   - Team feedback
   - Regular reviews

4. Share learning:
   - Team training
   - Knowledge transfer
   - Best practices
   - Success stories
   - Continuous improvement

A CLOSING NOTE FROM THE AUTHOR

Dear Reader,

Thank you for taking this journey with Sarah and me through the Four Pillars of Business Success. If you're feeling a mix of excitement and perhaps a little overwhelm right now, that's perfectly normal. Change, even positive change, can feel daunting when viewed as a whole.

Remember, Sarah didn't transform her business overnight. She started with small, manageable steps that gradually built into significant changes. Like Sarah, you don't need to implement everything at once. Start with one area that resonates most strongly with you - perhaps it's documenting your core processes, or maybe it's implementing a proper follow-up system. Choose one thing, make it work, then move on to the next.

The key is to start. Today. Not when you have more time (you won't find it), not when things are less busy (they won't be), not when you feel more ready (you'll never feel completely ready). Start now, start small, but start.

Throughout this book, we've explored the challenges that many business owners face. I know these challenges intimately because I've lived them myself and helped numerous business owners overcome them. The strategies and systems shared in this book aren't theoretical - they're battle-tested approaches that work in the real world.

Your business has the potential to be more than just a source of income; it can be a vehicle for personal growth, a creator of opportunities for others, and a legacy you can be proud of. But achieving this requires moving from working in your business to working on it. It requires building systems that allow your business to serve your life, rather than consume it.

If you're facing challenges in implementing any of the strategies we've discussed, or if you'd like to explore how the Four Pillars approach could work specifically in your business, please don't hesitate to reach out. You can contact me directly at paulflavin@growpartnership.co.uk. I genuinely want to see you succeed and am here to help.

Remember, every successful business owner started exactly where you are now. The difference between those who achieve their dreams and those who don't often comes down to one simple thing: taking action. You've already taken the first step by reading this book. Now it's time for the next step.

Trust in yourself, trust in the process, and begin your journey to building the business - and life - you've always wanted. You can do this, and you don't have to do it alone.

Wishing you every success,

Paul Flavin Founder, Grow Partnership
paulflavin@growpartnership.co.uk

P.S. I love hearing success stories from readers. As you implement these strategies and begin seeing results, please drop me a line and let me know how you're getting on. Your journey might just inspire another business owner to take their first step towards transformation.

ABOUT THE AUTHOR

Paul Flavin is a serial entrepreneur and award-winning business coach who learned success the hard way – through building, scaling, and selling several companies of his own. After a back injury ended his career as an Automotive Engineer, Paul navigated through various roles before a chance conversation on Southend Pier led him into financial services. Over two decades, he built and scaled multiple successful companies, experiencing both triumphs and setbacks that would later shape his coaching philosophy.

Working alongside his own business coach for 10 years gave Paul unique insight into both sides of the coaching relationship. This experience, combined with his hands-on success in scaling businesses, formed the foundation for his coaching career. Within just two years of becoming a business coach, Paul's results-driven approach earned him both National and International awards.

Now, as co-founder of GROW Partnership, Paul is on a mission to help one million business owners take control of their destiny through better knowledge and understanding. His practical, no-nonsense approach comes from having been in the trenches himself – he doesn't just teach theory, he shares battle-tested strategies that actually work.

Whether you're just starting out or looking to scale your existing business, Paul's insights will help you avoid the pitfalls and accelerate your journey to success.

Printed in Great Britain
by Amazon

61333915R00127